D1235957

The Negro
in Eighteenth-Century
Williamsburg

The Negro
in Eighteenth-Century
Williamsburg

By

THAD W. TATE

The
COLONIAL WILLIAMSBURG FOUNDATION
Williamsburg, Virginia

Library of Congress Catalogue Card Number 65-26599

ISBN 0-910412-29-4

*Distributed by the University
Press of Virginia*

Printed in the United States of America

Contents

Preface

The following study was completed initially in the spring of 1957 as a research report for the Colonial Williamsburg Foundation, with the idea that it would for the most part be used by the staff of that organization in whatever way it might serve to aid in the interpretation of restored Williamsburg. The decision to make it and a number of comparable studies of eighteenth-century Williamsburg more widely available in this present series is, as I understand it, intended to preserve in large measure the original format of a research report. For this reason I have not undertaken any extensive changes in my original manuscript. I have, however, made a few revisions, especially to take into account recent work on the origins of slavery, to incorporate additional evidence on the Negro school operated in Williamsburg under the auspices of the Associates of Dr. Bray, and to make use of new statistics on Negro population in the Virginia colony. Although further research would undoubtedly add additional details to my account, I do not believe that they would substantially alter the conclusions that I have reached.

In a sense, two approaches were possible in the preparation of this study of Williamsburg's Negro population in the colonial era. One alternative would have been a broad survey of what would really amount to slavery and the Negro in Tidewater Virginia. The other would confine itself as far as possible to Williamsburg and to the impact of town life on an element in the population whose initial reason for being here had been the performance of agricultural labor.

For the most part, I have attempted to follow the narrower approach. Many of the subjects in which it seemed likely Colonial Williamsburg would be most interested—the actual number of slaves in Williamsburg, the distribution of ownership, the work the slaves performed, their living conditions—

were precisely the features of slavery most likely to be modified by whatever urban characteristics Williamsburg possessed.

Certain other parts of the report, which touch matters of criminal law, runaways, religion, and education apply much more generally to town and plantation alike. Even here, however, I have tried to come as quickly as possible to their specific relevance to Williamsburg.

There are no doubt some omissions that may have arisen from this attempt to limit the scope of the report as far as possible to Williamsburg, and there is almost certainly much about plantation slave life that could have been useful in the interpretation of the eighteenth century that Colonial Williamsburg undertakes. However, a detailed investigation of plantation slavery in colonial Virginia, one that would really present new information, would constitute a project of major proportions without necessarily meeting the immediate need of specific information on Williamsburg. It might also, I think, increase rather than diminish the problem of the shortage of sources of information on an inarticulate part of the population.

Thanks to the excellent working collection of the Colonial Williamsburg Research Library, especially its holdings of microfilmed documents from many English and American depositories, I have had the novel experience of being able to complete this study largely in that library. The references in the bibliography will make it apparent, however, that I am indebted to a number of other libraries, whose librarians so willingly made parts of their collection available for microfilming and use by the staff of Colonial Williamsburg. I completed the original report, as the reader will infer from my earlier comments, while I was a member of the Colonial Williamsburg research staff myself, and I still carry many pleasant memories of the spirit of cooperation and stimulus to scholarship that prevailed among the community of fellow historians and other research staff members with whom I was then associated.

June, 1964   T. W. T.

A Note to the Third Printing

This third printing incorporates no changes in the text and annotation of *The Negro in Eighteenth-Century Williamsburg* beyond a few that were made to update some of the annotation in the second printing. The reason is by no means a lack of relevant new scholarship. Rather, the opposite is more nearly true: the recent published work has so altered some major interpretations of the history of blacks in early Virginia that it would require extensive rewriting to incorporate them in a fully satisfactory manner in the printed volume.

I might single out in particular three or four such points. First, there has been a marked shift away from interest in the early and mid-seventeenth-century origins of slavery as a legal institution in Virginia and the related issue of the presence of white racial antipathy as an ingredient in the development of black bondage. Few would question that slavery and racist attitudes made an early appearance in Virginia, but historians have of late been far more concerned with the development of black slavery as the major component of the Chesapeake labor system and with a correspondingly rapid increase in black population. Neither began to occur with significant force before the 1680s, and only then did the black presence in Virginia assume fundamental importance. This new emphasis seems especially evident, for example, in Edmund S. Morgan's *American Slavery, American Freedom: The Ordeal of Colonial Virginia,* a study that emphasizes the pervasive influence of slavery on the colony thereafter. Russell R. Menard's article, "From Servants to Slaves: The Transformation of the Chesapeake Labor System," which appeared in the Winter 1977 issue of *Southern Studies,* is also crucial for understanding this shift of emphasis.

A second, perhaps even more significant reinterpretation of the place of blacks in colonial Virginia reflects the increasing attention accorded the development of an Afro-American culture distinct from that of the dominant white population. It emphasizes in particular the extent to which blacks were able to carve out areas of independence in their lives despite the rigors of slavery—in family life and ties of kinship, in patterns of work, or in clandestine movement among neighboring plantations, to name a few examples. Although some of the major contours of this interpretation have been sketched in several articles by Allan Kulikoff, which are listed in the bibliography to this volume, several major studies that relate to the question are in press.

Black religion, another manifestation of a distinctive Afro-American culture, has long been a subject of investigation by numerous historians, but a renewed interest in the rise of late colonial evangelicalism has had an impact on black studies. This attention in the first instance perhaps derives as much from those who have been primarily concerned with evangelical religion as a social and cultural force among whites as from those primarily interested in black religion itself. Yet, in a work such as Rhys Isaac's *Transformation of Virginia, 1740–1790,* the author has demonstrated how much evangelical religion among blacks incorporated a sufficient number of African survivals to make it a principal component of Afro-American culture.

The evangelical movement among blacks and whites alike also coincided with and apparently bore an integral relationship to the outbreak of the American Revolution. Most Virginia blacks, for example, who gained freedom in the post-Revolutionary years owed their emancipation in large part to the religious convictions of masters who were caught up in evangelicalism at a time when it was still strongly antislavery. There are many reasons to reconsider the history of blacks during the Revolutionary era. In the process we might well give stronger emphasis in one way or another to a sense of restlessness and a consciousness of the desirability of liberty on the part of blacks, feelings that had religious no less than political roots.

I believe that much of what I said at an earlier time about the extent and timing of black population growth in Virginia, about the degree of independence and sense of community that life in the semiurban setting of Williamsburg seemed to afford its resident blacks, and about the potential impact of Christianity and of the American Revolution on slaves is generally compatible with some of these new directions in black historiography, if not so clearly spelled out as I might now try to put it. I believe, too, that the detailed information I sought to present about blacks in the specific setting of Williamsburg has not in the meantime been greatly extended or corrected. At least one question has been raised as to whether my population estimates, in which I judged blacks to comprise half the population of Williamsburg on the eve of the Revolution, may be too high. It is likely that such a proportion did not develop any earlier than the mid-eighteenth century, but from post-1750 inventories of some Williamsburg estates, from the frequency of newspaper advertisements concerning Williamsburg blacks, from a census total for 1775, and from what we can infer from more precise population figures for the 1780s I am inclined to stand by my admittedly rough estimate for the late colonial era.

Since I think, then, that the Williamsburg data hold up reasonably well and can be fitted into some of the newer and more penetrating interpretations of the history of blacks in Virginia, I hope this study can stand in large part as it was originally written and be seen as what it is, a product of a certain time and stage of scholarship in what still remains a rapidly evolving field of study.

I have, however, sought in this printing to revise and expand the bibliography to incorporate references to much of the recent work. Even such a current listing cannot, however, suggest what an impressive body of additional work is at the moment on the threshold of publication. Anyone interested in the subject should know that its bibliography will soon include, among other examples of new work, a significant comparative study of Afro-American culture in colonial South Carolina and Virginia by Philip Morgan; a book by Allan Kulikoff, *Tobacco and Slaves,* that will draw his extensive research on blacks even more fully into the general social and economic history of the eighteenth-century Chesapeake; Douglas Deal's examination of free blacks in the social and ethnic setting of the early Eastern Shore region; and Philip Schwarz's exhaustive investigation of slave crime and its punishment in the colony. We can expect, too, that the forthcoming edition of *Virginia Slave-Trade Statistics 1698–1775,* edited by Walter Minchinton, Celia King, and Peter White, will add extensively to the data included in the earlier documentary work on the slave trade by Elizabeth Donnan and thereby enlarge our understanding of the impact of the overseas slave trade on Virginia.

Since it seems likely, however, that Williamsburg during the years when it was the capital of the colony will continue to provide a somewhat unusual environment for black life—different certainly from plantation agricultural slavery of the same era and different as well from southern urban slavery of succeeding eras—I hope that the present study, used in conjunction with the more recent work, may still contribute to our understanding of one strand of a complex subject.

T.W.T.

The Negro
in Eighteenth-Century
Williamsburg

CHAPTER I

The Seventeenth Century:
The Emergence of Slavery

ALMOST everyone who has even the slightest knowledge of the history of colonial Virginia inevitably recalls the year 1619 for three events. In addition to the first meeting of a representative assembly in the New World and the arrival of a shipload of marriageable maidens, the third occurrence was, of course, the landing of a cargo of Negroes in the James River, the first to be imported to the North American continent. The coming of these Negroes, twenty-odd in all, was almost certainly accidental. They were aboard a Dutch frigate which touched Virginia in late August after a plundering expedition in West Indian waters. Arriving at Point Comfort, the Dutch captain struck a bargain with the governor and the cape merchant to leave the blacks in exchange for sorely needed food. Not much later the *Treasurer,* a vessel fitted out in Virginia, left a single Negro in the colony.[1]

Although scholars have in some cases been insisting on the opposite for better than a half century, popular understanding has all too often continued to embrace some questionable assumptions about these first Negroes. It has been all but

1. There are accounts of the landing of the first Negroes in virtually every general history of seventeenth-century Virginia. Probably the most useful, because of its superior documentation, is that in James Curtis Ballagh, *A History of Slavery in Virginia* (Baltimore, 1902), pp. 7-9. The pertinent sources include Susan Myra Kingsbury, ed., *The Records of the Virginia Company of London* (Washington, 1906-1935), 3: 243; Edward Arber, ed., *Travels and Works of Captain John Smith* (Edinburgh, 1910), 2: 541-42. There is a very perceptive reconsideration of the first arrival in Wesley Frank Craven's *White, Red, and Black: The Seventeenth-Century Virginian* (Charlottesville, Va., 1971), p. 77ff., and also in his "Twenty Negroes to Jamestown in 1619?" *Virginia Quarterly Review,* 47(1971): 416-20. Craven questions convincingly some details of the traditional account that I have generally followed.

impossible to correct the impressions that slavery immediately became a precise, legally defined institution; that the white colonists just as quickly saw the Africans as a solution to the pressing labor shortage of the colony; and that, as a consequence, a rapidly swelling wave of slave labor began to flow into Virginia from 1619 on. Such viewpoints deserve to be suspect for their insistent note of immediacy, if nothing else. The processes of history normally move more slowly, and the emergence of slavery in Virginia is no exception. Awareness of the economic usefulness of slave labor, the importation of Negroes in quantity, and the legal recognition of slavery were not instantaneous consequences of what happened in the year 1619.

These first Negroes came into a society in which an unfree status, that of the indentured servant, was already well known. Since the twenty on board the Dutch frigate were acquired by the governor and the cape merchant in exchange for public stores, they presumably took their place alongside the other servants of the London Company.[2] Over the next four years these twenty, plus three or four others who were brought in on other ships, became scattered out to several of the settlements in the colony, where they were in the possession of some seven different men, most of whom were officers in the government.[3]

Thus was established a pattern of indentured servitude for Negroes which continued until about mid-century.[4] Like other

2. *Records of Virginia Company*, 3: 243.
3. Ballagh, *Slavery in Virginia*, pp. 29-30.
4. Perhaps the most comprehensive recent statement of the gradually emerging character of Negro slavery is Oscar and Mary F. Handlin, "Origins of the Southern Labor System," *William and Mary Quarterly*, 3rd series, 7 (April, 1950): 199-222. A briefer statement can be found in John Hope Franklin, *From Slavery to Freedom: A History of American Negroes* (New York, 1948), pp. 70-72. Ballagh, *Slavery in Virginia*, pp. 27-90, first established the slow development of slavery in a legal sense. John Henderson Russell, *The Free Negro in Virginia, 1619-1865* (Baltimore, 1913), p. 23ff., also supports the evolution of Negro slavery from indentured servitude.

There are, however, some modern historians who challenge this view and who regard slavery as having been the status of Negroes almost from the moment of their importation into Virginia. This is true of Susie M. Ames, *Studies of the Virginia Eastern Shore in the Seventeenth Century*

servants the Negroes completed a period of service and became freemen. Some of them became landowners and masters of other servants. One of the best known of these was Anthony Johnson, who had apparently reached Virginia in 1621 and had within a year or two gained his freedom. Johnson then married Mary, a Negro woman who came on the *Margett and John* in 1622. He began to acquire property and to import Negro servants of his own, until he had developed a small African community in Northampton County.[5] One of Anthony Johnson's former Negro servants, Richard Johnson, a carpenter, was even able to import two white servants for whom he received the customary headrights of fifty acres.[6] There are a number of other instances of Negroes who before 1660 acquired land on headrights, by lease, or through purchase.[7]

The word "slave" does appear from time to time before the 1660s, but there is no way to prove that it had a meaning in law. Rather, it was a popular expression of the rigorous demands of servitude, applied to Negro and white alike, as in the case of the poor planters who complained that their children were being held as "slaves or drudges" for the debts of their parents.[8]

Gradually, however, in the period roughly between 1640 and 1660 the Negro's status in Virginia society began to decline and white and Negro servants were no longer approximate equals. In time the Negro found himself in lifetime bondage. The

(Richmond, Va., 1940), p. 100ff., and Wesley Frank Craven, *The Southern Colonies in the Seventeenth Century, 1607-1689* (Baton Rouge, La., 1949), p. 402. Another statement of this view occurs in a paper given by Robert D. Ronsheim at the 1956 meeting of the Southern Historical Association and summarized in *Journal of Southern History*, 23 (Feb., 1957): 79. Mr. Ronsheim viewed as more important, however, the relationship of plantation size to labor force and the determination of when large plantations directly affected the labor system.

5. *The Negro in Virginia*. Compiled by the Writers' Program of the Work Projects Administration (New York, 1940), pp. 11-12.

6. Ibid., p. 11.

7. Ibid. See also James H. Brewer, "Negro Property Owners in Seventeenth-Century Virginia," *William and Mary Quarterly*, 3rd ser., 12 (Oct., 1955):575-80.

8. For a fuller treatment of the colloquial usage of the term slave, see Handlins, "Southern Labor System," pp. 203-4.

precise rate at which this subjection of the black man occurred as well as the reasons why it happened are subjects of dispute among historians. In large part the disagreement becomes one over whether slavery followed from racial prejudice or whether racial prejudice gripped whites only as a consequence of the enslavement of the Negro. Those who place the appearance of legalized slavery comparatively late, that is, no earlier than 1660, argue that the white colonists were originally without prejudice, developing it only when they came to know the Negro in bondage. On the other hand, those who believe that slavery developed more rapidly, existing in custom and recognized by the courts in individual instances at least by 1640, conclude that immediate antipathy toward the Negro served to bring on his decline. In truth, the argument focuses on a comparatively brief period—twenty years at the most—during which evidence of the legal recognition of slavery and of racial feeling appear more or less simultaneously. There seems to be little reason not to believe that the two factors, rather than presenting a distinct order of causality, might not have reacted upon each other, "dynamically joining hands to hustle the Negro down the road to complete degradation."[9]

9. The conclusion that slavery and prejudice developed simultaneously rests particularly on the work of Winthrop P. Jordan, who first made the point in "Modern Tensions and the Origins of American Slavery," *Journal of Southern History*, 28 (Feb., 1962):29, and restated it in his monumental *White over Black: American Attitudes toward the Negro, 1550-1812* (Chapel Hill, N.C., 1968), pp. 71-82. The principal contemporary spokesman for the late development of slavery are the Handlins, "Southern Labor System," and Kenneth M. Stampp, *The Peculiar Institution: Slavery in the Ante-Bellum South* (New York, 1956), pp. vii-viii, 3-33. Carl N. Degler presents the case for early racial prejudice as a cause of slavery in "Slavery and the Genesis of American Race Prejudice," *Comparative Studies in Society and History*, 2 (Oct., 1959): 49-66, and also in his *Out of the Past: The Forces that Shaped Modern America* (New York, 1959), pp. 26-39. See also the works by Susie M. Ames and Wesley F. Craven, cited in note 4 above. It seems fair to say that, as this historical controversy has continued, the view that racial antipathy toward blacks was present from the first has gained overwhelming support. For example, Alden T. Vaughan, "Blacks in Virginia: A Note on the First Decade," to be published in the forthcoming July issue of the *William and Mary Quarterly*, will offer additional evidence of discrimination against the first black arrivals.

In some part, however, legal slavery may have emerged as the result of increasing pressure to define length and conditions of service for white settlers. In the first years of the colony formal indentures were not the rule, and many persons spent long, indefinite periods as servants.[10] Eventually, in order to assure a continuing flow of indentured labor, it became necessary to write into law strict limitations on servitude that held out the hope of life as a freeman and landowner. The initial statute in Virginia was one of 1642/43 fixing the limits of service for persons arriving without indentures at four years for those over the age of 20, five years for those from 12 to 20, and seven years for children under 12.[11] This law applied specifically to English servants, but subsequent modifications guaranteed a fixed term for all white Christians, no matter from where they came.[12]

The Negro servant, however, was another case. His coming was involuntary, and his bargaining power nonexistent. It became clearer and clearer to white masters that there was no reason for releasing a Negro servant in a few years and every advantage in claiming his labor indefinitely. Thus, in the same decades of the 1640s and 1650s in which the term of indenture for whites was becoming fixed and short, the Negro was coming to be regarded as a "servant for life."

The lifetime service of many Negroes was at first a matter of custom rather than law, but court decisions recognizing the principle were becoming more frequent. The earliest known case involved three runaway servants, one a Negro, who were recovered in Maryland and brought to trial in 1640. The two white men had their time of service extended by a year plus three years of labor on public works, but the Negro was ordered to serve for the balance of his life.[13] The fate of Manuel, a

10. Handlins, "Southern Labor System," pp. 209-10.

11. William Waller Hening, ed., *The Statutes at Large Being a Collection of all the Laws of Virginia* (Richmond, Va., etc. 1810-1823), 1:257.

12. Ibid., 1: 411, 441-42, 538-39; 2: 113-14, 169, 297.

13. Helen T. Catterall, ed., *Judicial Cases Concerning American Slavery and the Negro* (Washington, 1924-1926), 1: 77. E. Franklin Frazier, *The Negro in the United States* (New York, 1949), pp. 23-24. Philip Alexander Bruce, *Economic History of Virginia in the Seventeenth Century* (New York, 1895-1907), 2:23.

mulatto who had been bought "as a Slave for Ever" in September, 1644, and then was adjudged not to be a slave and freed in 1665, was an exception; but it indicates the prevailing trend.[14] Another example concerns the same Anthony Johnson who had established on the Eastern Shore a colony of Negroes indentured to him. In 1653 Johnson was involved in a suit brought by one of his men, John Casor, over the length of time for which Casor was obligated. Johnson succeeded in making good his claim to the man's service for life.[15]

The first recognition in statutory law of this state of affairs occurred in March, 1660/61. At that, this law was no more than an oblique recognition that life servitude was now a *possibility* for some Negroes; for it was enacted to deal with English servants who might "run away in company with any negroes who are incapable of making satisfaction by addition of time."[16]

Besides the widening gap in the length of service demanded of white and Negro servants, a few other distinctions began to appear in these years to the disadvantage of the black man. These restrictions bear some of the marks of racial prejudice. Negroes were excluded, for instance, by a statute of January, 1639/40 from the requirement of possessing arms and ammunition.[17] Three years later Negro women servants, but not white women servants, were counted as tithables for purposes of taxation.[18] And in 1641 the outcome of a suit brought by a Negro servant to confirm his ownership of some hogs suggested that Negroes, even when indentured for a fixed time, were more

14. Catterall, *Judicial Cases*, 1: 58-59; *Negro in Virginia*, pp. 13-14; "Randolph Manuscript." *Virginia Magazine of History and Biography*, 17 (July, 1909):232.

15. *Negro in Virginia*, pp. 11-12; Frazier, *Negro in the United States*, p. 25.

16. Hening, *Statutes*, 2:26. Any English servant found guilty under this act was to have time equal to the Negro's absence added to his term of servitude. The same law was re-enacted in the following March (1661/2); ibid., 2:117.

17. Ibid., 1:226.

18. Ibid., 1:242. Bruce, *Economic History of Virginia*, 2:101-2, regards this as not a matter of racial discrimination but a reflection of the use of Negro women largely as field hands and also of the desire not to discourage in any way the emigration of white women servants. Nonetheless, it served to set the Negro apart in some sense.

closely restricted than whites in their right to possess personal property.[19]

Once the law of 1660/61 had admitted the possibility of life servitude, there followed a period lasting down to about 1675 or 1680 during which a number of laws confirmed or defined further the Negro's lower status. More and more, these differentiations cut the Negro "apart from all other servants and gave a new depth to his bondage."[20] By 1670, for instance, the laws of the colony clearly sought to make service for life the *normal* condition under which Negroes would in the future be introduced into Virginia.[21]

One step in this progressive decline of the Negro's position was the elimination of Christianity as a factor which might ameliorate his servitude. The seventeenth century was inclined to take seriously the proposition that conversion entitled heathen servants to liberty.[22] The fact was not lost on Virginians, however, that a literal application of this principle could undermine the whole structure of perpetual servitude which had so recently evolved. The General Assembly as early as 1667 eased the concern of owners of Negroes already in the colony by decreeing that baptism "doth not alter the condition of the person as to his bondage or ffreedome."[23]

Sealing off Christianity as a means of freedom for Negroes yet to be imported could not be altered so directly, however. There was still a reluctance to legislate frankly along color lines, and the first attempt to insure life service for new Negroes drew the simple religious test of heathen and Christian on the assumption that most of the Negroes would certainly be unconverted. This occurred in the law of 1670 already cited in connection with life servitude. It stated that "all servants not being christians imported into this colony by shipping" were to be "slaves for their lives."[24] A certain number of Christianized Negroes escaped with short indentures under this enactment;

19. Catterall, *Judicial Cases*, 1: 57-58.
20. Handlins, "Southern Labor System," p. 209.
21. Hening, *Statutes*, 2: 283.
22. Ballagh, *Slavery in Virginia*, p. 46; Handlins, "Southern Labor System," p. 212.
23. Hening, *Statutes*, 2: 260.
24. Ibid., p. 283.

but a 1682 law partially closed the loophole by denying eventual freedom to servants whose parentage and native country were not Christian and who were not themselves Christian at the time of their first purchase.[25] This was a test few of the new arrivals could meet. The 1705 act which codified much of the existing law on slaves and servants restated this formula a little more directly by declaring all servants imported into Virginia, except Turks and Moors, who were not Christian in their native country or who were not free in a Christian country should be held as slaves, regardless of any later conversion to Christianity.[26] In effect, then, Christianity ceased to shield the newly imported Negro from slavery, just as it had not after 1667 offered any hope of freedom to those who were already here.

Another direct result of perpetual servitude was an alteration in the methods of determining status for Negro children. There had always been a problem about the illegitimate offspring of all bound servants. Now, however, the former legislation which depended principally on additional terms of service—by the mother to compensate her master for time lost during pregnancy and by the father to compensate the parish for care of the child—could no longer apply to most Negro parents.[27] Where both parents were Negroes serving for life, the necessity for punishment, as a matter of fact, ceased to exist. By custom children born of such a union assumed the status of the parents and became permanent and, in time, welcome additions to their owner's labor force. If only one parent were a Negro, however, determination of the child's status became more complicated. Here Virginia early arrived at the solution that children born in the colony should "be held bond or free only according to the condition of the mother."[28] An illegitimate offspring of a mulatto mother, on the other hand, served as an indentured laborer and eventually became free.[29]

Whatever may have been the custom of the day, the law

25. Ibid., p. 491.
26. Ibid., 3:447-48.
27. Ibid., 1:438; 2:114, 168; 3:139.
28. Ibid., 2:170. This was enacted in 1662.
29. Ibid., 4:133.

continued during these years to regard the Negro's personal rights as substantially those of any other servant. Statutory law sometimes employed the word slave, but nearly always so that it read clearly in the context of servant for life.[30] It is arguable that the distinction between being a servant for life and a chattel slave was of no practical advantage; yet there was a difference. For one thing, there was less difficulty about the possibility of gaining freedom.[31] Also, the courts were more inclined to deal with a servant, even one bound perpetually, as a man rather than as a species of property.

During the last quarter of the century, however, the status of the Negro in the eyes of the law began to change once more. His personal rights were reduced to a minimum and he was left as a true chattel slave.[32] Thus, it was comparatively late in the seventeenth century before slavery became fixed in the form in which we know it in the eighteenth and nineteenth centuries.

Now there appeared rudimentary "black codes," the first of the laws controlling the conduct, freedom of movement, and personal rights of Negroes that were to become so common a feature of slavery. A 1680 statute, ostensibly enacted to prevent insurrection but in actual practice designed to curb freedom of movement and resistance to a white man, marked the effective beginning of these regulations. Subsequent laws soon established trial procedures which differed from those for white servants.[33]

30. Ibid., 2: 260, 283, 299, 491. In particular, the 1670 law speaks of "slaves for their lives" and that of 1672, of "any negroe, molatto, Indian slave, or servant for life."

31. Bruce, *Economic History of Virginia*, 2: 124.

32.   The 1669 law (Hening, *Statutes*, 2: 270) providing that the killing of a Negro under correction was not a felony is a somewhat earlier example of a loss of an important legal protection by the Negro. However, the reasoning of the preamble was that a Negro could not serve additional time as a punishment, hence corporal punishment was the only disciplinary force available, and that the master might therefore have to be protected from the consequences of corporal punishment which killed a Negro. In that sense, the law was primarily a consequence of lifetime servitude.

33. Hening, *Statutes*, 2: 481-82, 492-93; 3: 86-88, 102-3. The subject of colonial "black codes" is developed at greater length below, Chapter X, sec. 1.

Color now became the determining factor of slavery. Though there had undoubtedly been much racial antipathy toward Negroes almost from the beginning, the Virginians seemed in no hurry to write it into law.[34] The first law in which "Negro" was clearly used to show racial feeling rather than to distinguish two types of bound labor was perhaps the 1670 enactment forbidding free Negroes and Indians to own white servants.[35] The first act on Negro insurrections in 1680 carried the feeling a step further by punishing the black man who should "presume to lift up his hand in opposition against any christian," and the perpetual banishment after 1691 of any white who married a Negro or mulatto more or less completed the circle.[36] Yet, as late as 1705, in defining slave status the law still clung to the elaborate fiction of heathen birth rather than color.[37] But by this time everyone must have known color was the real badge of slavery.

The last door of escape from a lifetime of slavery was closed against the Negro in 1691, when owners were forbidden to free a slave except by transporting him from the colony within six months.[38] Except for a handful of slaves freed by special acts of the General Assembly the practical possibility of manumission had virtually ceased to exist.

From a legal point of view perhaps the final step in reducing a human to the level of slavery is to say point-blank that he has ceased to be a man and has become a species of property. In Virginia this was foreshadowed as early as 1669.[39] In 1705 the Assembly stated explicitly that "all negro, mulatto, and Indian slaves, in all courts of judicature, and other places, within this dominion, shall be held, taken, and adjudged to be real estate . . ."[40] There was an attempt in 1748 to make slaves personal rather than real property, but it was part of a law which

34. Ibid., 1: 146, 552; Handlins, "Southern Labor System," p. 216.
35. Hening, *Statutes*, 1:280-81.
36. Ibid., 2: 481; 3: 87.
37. Ibid., 447-48.
38. Ibid., 87-88.
39. By the law exempting masters from punishment for killing a slave under correction, it being presumed the owner would not willfully destroy his own estate. Ibid., 2: 270. See also: 2: 288.
40. Ibid., 3: 333.

received the royal disallowance.[41] It was difficult to apply the principle that the slave was mere property in every case, however; and in practice both law and custom were forced from time to time to recognize the slave as a person.[42] But the fact remains that in becoming a slave the Negro had become a piece of property first and a man only secondarily.

If the development of slavery was such a slow process, requiring almost until the end of the seventeenth century to reach its final stage, then the assumption that the colonial planters immediately saw the Negro as an ideal answer to such problems as the chronic labor shortage and the rigorous heat of the southern climate becomes untenable.[43] In fact, the colonists continued for some time to prefer white labor, even with the disadvantage of short indentures. Much of the degradation in status of the Negro may have come about because the planters wanted white labor and set out to make the terms of indentured service more attractive. Lacking similar bargaining power, the Negro was more or less caught in the backwash.[44] Not even the extension of the headright system to Negroes in 1635 had any immediate effect on the number of Negroes imported, for only in the last ten years of the century did the patent books record more than a thousand African headrights in any decade.[45]

It is also absolutely fundamental to any understanding of this formative period to remember how small the Negro population of Virginia actually was before 1680 or 1690. It may be more than coincidence that the appearance of true slavery and the beginning of a sizeable influx of Negroes into Virginia coincide

41. Ibid., 5: 432-33.

42. Ballagh, *Slavery in Virginia*, p. 96ff., though the case for the personal rights of the slave is considerably overstated.

43. For an expression of this older, deterministic view see Bruce, *Economic History of Virginia*, 2: 57ff. It is also an important theme in the work of Ulrich B. Phillips.

44. Handlins, "Southern Labor System," pp 206-8; Stampp, *The Peculiar Institution*, pp. 1-3; Craven, *Southern Colonies in the Seventeenth Century*, pp. 25, 214-15.

45. *Negro in Virginia*, p. 4; Bruce, *Economic History of Virginia*, 2: 85; *William and Mary Quarterly*, 1st ser., 7 (April, 1899), 281-87; Craven, *White, Red, and Black*, pp. 82-87.

so closely. From the first arrival to the beginning of the last quarter of the century there was never more than an occasional importation of Negroes. The census of 1624-1625 counted only 23. In 1648 an estimate listed 300 "Negro servants" as compared with 15,000 white settlers, the Negroes being no more than two percent of the colony's total population. By Governor Berkeley's estimate in 1671, Negroes comprised about four percent of the total, or 2,000 out of a population of 48,000.[46]

Over the decade of the 1670s the black population rose another thousand to 3,000.[47] By 1700 there were about 16,390 Negro inhabitants of Virginia.[48] Thus, the closing thirty years of the seventeenth century saw a small, but significant, step-up in the arrival of Negroes; but the mass importations belong to the eighteenth century.

As the new century opened, there was no doubt that slavery had become a fixed, legally defined institution in the colony of Virginia. The use of Negro labor was, moreover, finding wider acceptance, and larger importations of slaves were beginning to occur. The way stood open for the enormous extension of slavery which occurred in the first half of the eighteenth century.

46. All the above figures are collected in Evarts B. Greene and Virginia D. Harrington, *American Population Before the Federal Census of 1790* (New York, 1932), p. 136.

47. *Ibid.*, p. 137.

48. I have used the estimates of Negro population in U.S. Bureau of the Census, *Historical Statistics of the United States: Colonial Times to 1957* (Washington, 1960), p. 756. With figures of 9,345 in 1690 and 16,390 in 1700 these estimates are larger than many previous ones for these two decades, but they agree with the older figures for all the earlier decades. Craven, *White, Red, and Black*, pp. 82-103, reviews the difficult problem of determining black population and concludes that the total at the end of the century was "somewhat larger but not greatly in excess of six thousand."

CHAPTER II

The Eighteenth Century:
The Growth of Slavery

T HE 16,390 Negroes residing in Virginia in 1700 had grown
to 26,559 by 1720, to 30,000 by 1730, or almost double the 1700
figure. In the next decade—the 1730s—the Negro population
doubled once again, reaching an estimated 60,000.[1] It was not
long until annual importations of Negroes had climbed to a
peak of three or four thousand a year, while the number of
Virginia-born Negroes increased correspondingly.[2]

By mid-century the estimates of population varied widely,
but Governor Dinwiddie's 1756 figures were perhaps as reliable
as any. Estimating from the count of tithables, he arrived at a
total population in Virginia of 293,472, of which 173,316 were
white and 120,156 Negro. By the 1760s the proportion of white
to Negro was not quite half and half, a ratio which remained
more or less constant to the end of the eighteenth century. As
was to be expected, the highest density of Negroes occurred in
the Tidewater, but slaves were also numerous in the Piedmont.
Only in the Valley and in the mountain areas was the Negro
population really small.[3]

This rapid increase did not depend alone on the willingness
of the colonial planters to employ Negro labor. It also demand-

1. U.S. Bureau of the Census, *Historical Statistics of the United
States: Colonial Times to 1957* (Washington, 1960), p. 756; Evarts B.
Greene and Virginia D. Harrington, *American Population Before the
Federal Census of 1790* (New York, 1932), p. 139; Lawrence H. Gipson,
The British Empire before the American Revolution (Caldwell, Idaho,
and New York, 1936-1970), 2:107.

2. Lewis Cecil Gray, *History of Agriculture in the Southern United
States to 1860* (New York, 1941), 1:355.

3. Greene and Harrington, *American Population*, pp. 139-143. *Historical Abstracts of the United States*, p. 756.

13

ed the evolution of an efficient, large-scale slave trade.[4] Through much of the seventeenth century sporadic Dutch trading activity was responsible for most of the importations of Negroes.[5] The Virginia Assembly attempted to encourage this trade in 1659 by exempting Dutch merchants from paying ten shillings per hogshead duty on tobacco received for Negroes, permitting them to pay instead the two shillings English duty.[6]

English mercantile interests did not become actively involved in the African slave trade until the Restoration. In 1662 the Company of Royal Adventurers Trading to Africa received a monopoly of the slave trade. This company, however, survived for only ten difficult years and never recorded a contract for supplying Virginia with Negroes.[7] In 1672 a new company, the Royal African Company, received a charter which passed along to it the monopoly of the slave trade to the English colonies. There has been a tendency to assume too easily that the company was able to take full advantage of its favored position.[8] In reality, the Royal African Company found it difficult

4. Philip D. Curtin, *The Atlantic Slave Trade: A Census* (Madison, Wis., 1969), deals with the trade generally; there are specific references to the Virginia trade at pp. 118 and 143-44. Important for the Virginia trade specifically are Charles W. Killinger, "The Royal African Company Slave Trade to Virginia, 1689-1713" (unpublished M.A. thesis, College of William and Mary, 1969) and Elizabeth Suttell, "The British Slave Trade to Virginia, 1698-1728" (unpublished M.A. thesis, College of William and Mary, 1965). Many of the most important documents on the Virginia trade are assembled in Elizabeth Donnan, ed., *Documents Illustrative of the Slave Trade to America* (Washington, 1935), 4:2-7, 49-234.

5. Gray, *Agriculture in the Southern United States,* 1: 353; Wesley Frank Craven, *White, Red, and Black: The Seventeenth-Century Virginian* (Charlottesville, Va., 1971), pp. 89-91, cautions that the extent of Dutch involvement may be overestimated.

6. William Waller Hening, ed., *The Statutes at Large Being a Collection of all the Laws of Virginia* (Richmond, Va., etc., 1810-1823), 1: 540.

7. Gray, *Agriculture in the Southern United States,* 1: 352.

8. James Curtis Ballagh, *A History of Slavery in Virginia* (Baltimore, 1902), p. 10; Philip Alexander Bruce, *Economic History of Virginia in the Seventeenth Century* (New York, 1895-1907), 2: 78, 82. The standard history of the Royal African Company is Kenneth G. Davies, *The Royal African Company* (New York, 1957).

to protect itself against interlopers from both England and the colonies. Not even the support of the Crown, which consistently instructed royal governors to give all possible encouragement to the company, could help.[9] The Royal African Company contracted on several occasions in the 1670s for shipments of Negroes to Virginia and made some deliveries.[10] But, even though Governor Culpeper's statement that the company had never sold slaves in the colony was obviously an exaggeration, the Royal African Company was unsuccessful in dominating the Virginia market.[11]

Some of the challengers of the company monopoly seemed to have established good local connections in Virginia through men like the first William Byrd and William Fitzhugh. In the 1680s Byrd was interested in a number of transactions that involved bringing in small shipments of Negroes from the West Indies.[12] About the same time Fitzhugh was in correspondence with a New England merchant about the details of trading tobacco for slaves.[13]

Ultimately, in 1698, the Royal African Company lost its monopoly, being forced to give way to an arrangement which permitted "separate traders" to carry slaves by paying certain duties to the company.[14] Other merchants could now openly compete, sending their vessels, among other places, to the landings and ports which dotted the Virginia rivers. The figures for 1699-1708, which show that the separate traders carried 5,692 Negroes to Virginia and the Royal African Company 679, are a clear indication of the weak position of the company in the trade.[15] After these years shipments of slaves by the company became increasingly intermittent, though there were still a

9. Donnan, *Documents*, 4: 5, 55-56.
10. Ibid., pp. 53-55; Ballagh, *Slavery in Virginia*, p. 13. Killinger, "Royal African Company Slave Trade to Virginia," provides a detailed treatment.
11. Donnan, *Documents*. 4: 5-6, 58.
12. "Letters of William Byrd, First," *Virginia Magazine of History and Biography*, 24 (1916): 229, 232; 25 (1917): 50, 52, 133.
13. "Letters of William Fitzhugh," *Virginia Magazine*, 1 (Oct., 1893): 108.
14. Gray, *Agriculture in the Southern United States*, 1: 353.
15. Donnan, *Documents*, 4:172-73.

few to Virginia in the 1720s.[16] Then, after 1730, it no longer shipped Negroes from the African coast.[17] The flow of slaves continued, however, with Bristol and Liverpool merchants dominating the trade. A sprinkling of New England vessels also brought slave cargoes from Africa, and a number of Virginia ships were employed to bring small groups of Negroes from the West Indies into the colony.[18]

As the century progressed, new Negroes were sold farther and farther up the rivers, until settlements on the Fall Line like Rocky Ridge, across the James from Richmond, became the most important slave markets in the colony. There was also a domestic trade in Virginia-born Negroes, prized for their greater skill and adjustment to white civilization and therefore commanding higher prices.[19]

As much as they had come to value slave labor, Virginians viewed these large-scale importations of Negroes with misgivings.[20] No one has yet managed a completely satisfactory explanation of why the colonists began to wish they could put some limit on the number of slaves to be introduced into the colony. An older generation of Virginia historians claimed to find evidence of moral and humanitarian objections to the trade in human beings.[21] Some of them have even charged that slaves were forced on the southern colonies by the pressure of greedy British and New England mercantile groups.[22] Any close reading of the evidence quickly suggests how little support there is for this point of view, whether it be the prevailing attitudes of most of the planters toward the Negro or in the fact that no cargo of healthy slaves ever lacked for purchasers. It is clear

16. Ibid., 4:184-85.

17. Gray, *Agriculture in the Southern United States,* 1:353-54.

18. Donnan, *Documents,* 4: 188-234, *passim.*

19. Marcus W. Jernegan, *Laboring and Dependent Classes in Colonial America, 1607-1783* (Chicago, 1931), pp. 8-9.

20. John Hope Franklin, *From Slavery to Freedom: A History of American Negroes* (New York, 1948), p. 72; Ballagh, *Slavery in Virginia,* p. 11.

21. Ibid.

22. This was a favorite theme, for example, of Lyon G. Tyler and one which he could contrive to inject into a discussion of virtually any subject.

that much less idealistic reasons were responsible for the planters' objections.

For one thing, social control of the Negro played a large part in the increasing uneasiness of the whites. Fear of slave insurrection became a daily fact of life in Virginia, and ultimately the slave owners came to feel that there must be a limit beyond which the proportion of Negroes in the population could not safely go. An economic factor was also involved. Often the explanation has been that owners of Negroes already in Virginia had a speculative interest in keeping additional African Negroes out in order to assure a steady increase in the value of their own human property. What seems more convincing, however, is the fact that many planters opposed the further drain of money and increase in colonial indebtedness that the purchase of African slaves necessarily imposed. Prosperity in the slave trade was directly related to economic conditions of the tobacco market with the result that it suffered some of the same consequences of overextended credit. The more perceptive colonists were fully aware of the connection.[23]

The principal strategem which the leaders of the colony evolved for discouraging too rapid an increase in the number of slaves was an import duty on African slaves that could be disguised as a revenue measure.[24] The long series of laws which enacted these duties began as early as 1699, and, for the first few years, were honestly intended to raise funds, rather than discourage trade. The initial act, for example, levied a charge of twenty shillings for each Negro imported specifically for the construction of the new Capitol at Williamsburg.[25] With one renewal this duty continued in force until late 1703.[26] After a

23. Jerman Baker to Duncan Rose, February 15, 1764, in *William and Mary Quarterly*, 1st ser., 12 (April, 1904): 242; Franklin, *From Slavery to Freedom*, pp. 72-73; Gray, *Agriculture in the Southern United States*, 1: 356.

24. Ibid., 356-57; Ballagh, *Slavery in Virginia*, pp. 11-24; Donnan, *Documents*, 4:7. There is a full and perceptive account of the slave duties in Darold D. Wax, "Negro Import Duties in Colonial Virginia: A Study of British Commercial Policy and Local Public Policy," *Virginia Magazine of History and Biography*, 79 (1971):29-45.

25. Hening, *Statutes*, 3: 193.

26. Ibid., 3: 212-13.

three month interval in early 1704 during which no duty was in effect, the impost was revived in April, 1704.[27] From then until 1718 some form of duty was in force without an important break. The tendency to make the duties prohibitory in character also began to appear, for during these years the amount climbed as high as £5 per Negro.[28]

From 1718 to 1723 the Assembly made no attempt to continue the duty.[29] Then, in 1723 an attempt to restore it at the rate of 40 shillings touched off the first organized opposition from English traders. The flood of petitions and representations by these men carried enough political weight to persuade the King to disallow the 1723 law and all subsequent attempts of the assembly to pass a duty over the next nine years.[30]

By a change of tactics that made a five percent *ad valorem* duty payable by the prospective buyer rather than by the importer the General Assembly broke the deadlock in 1732.[31] Thereafter and until the outbreak of the Revolution an *ad valorem* duty on slaves was in effect in Virginia, except for six months during 1751. The five percent rate of 1732 was gradually increased, until it stood at twenty percent during part of the French and Indian War. The whole effort to discourage the foreign slave trade led ultimately to the unsuccessful petition of the assembly in 1772 for a complete end to further importations and to the successful prohibition of the trade by the new state government in 1778.[32] But these events are more logically a part of the American Revolution in Virginia. Down to the outbreak of that struggle African slavers and West Indian traders continued to land their human cargoes in the colony with but little discouragement.

The role which the African Negroes and their American-born descendants assumed in plantation society possesses a certain

27. Ibid., 225, 229-35.
28. Ibid., 482; 4: 30; Ballagh, *Slavery in Virginia*, p. 15n.
29. Ibid., p. 16.
30. Donnan, *Documents*, 4: 102-27; Ballagh, *Slavery in Virginia*, pp. 16-17; Hening, *Statutes*, 4: 118.
31. Ibid., 317-22.
32. Ballagh, *Slavery in Virginia*, pp. 19-23; Hening, *Statutes*, 4: 394, 471-73; 5: 28-31, 91-92, 160-61, 318-19; 6: 217-21, 353-54, 419, 466; 7: 81, 281, 363, 383, 639-42; 8: 190-92, 237-38, 336-38, 530-32.

familiarity. The fact that most histories of slavery leap so quickly to the nineteenth century, where the details of plantation life survive so much more abundantly, does place difficulties in the way of a full picture of the eighteenth. However, the general outlines of the work of the Negro slaves, of their daily existence, and of their immovable position at the bottom of a stratified colonial society seem clear enough.

The largest proportion of Negroes—men, women, and children—were field hands, assigned to growing tobacco and the other marketable crops the colony produced.[33] This was the real purpose for which slavery had evolved, and it represented the institution in its most impersonal, burdensome, and typical form. The account of the field slave's lot by J. F. D. Smyth, an English traveler in Virginia just before the Revolution, is admittedly an unflattering one and no more to be accepted uncritically than any other single observation; but it is probably accurate enough in its description of the working day:

. . . He [the slave] is called up in the morning at day break, and is seldom allowed time enough to swallow three mouthfuls of homminy, or hoecake, but is driven out immediately to the field to hard labour, at which he continues, without intermission, until noon. . . . About noon is the time he eats his dinner, and he is seldom allowed an hour for that purpose. . . .

They [*i.e.*, the slaves] then return to severe labour, which continues in the field until dusk in the evening, when they repair to the tobaccohouses, where each has his task in stripping alloted him, that employs him for some hours.[34]

33. There is a brief summary in *The Negro in Virginia* (New York, 1940), p. 58-66, a work compiled by the Writers' Program of the Work Projects Administration. Herbert S. Klein, *Slavery in the Americas: A Comparative Study of Virginia and Cuba* (Chicago, 1967), examines eighteenth-century Virginia slavery in considerable depth and adds an interesting comparative dimension. Gerald W. Mullin, *Flight and Rebellion: Slave Resistance in Eighteenth-Century Virginia* (New York, 1972), is an extremely important new study that is wider in its coverage than the title might suggest, since it focuses on the entire process of black acculturation in colonial Virginia.

34. "Smyth's Travels in Virginia, in 1773," *Virginia Historical Register,* 6 (April, 1853): 84-85. Smyth's description of the Negroes at work in the evening stripping tobacco would obviously apply only at harvest.

A smaller, but still significant number, of slaves fared somewhat better as household workers and personal servants of the master's family.[35] Almost invariably accounts of slaves who enjoyed especially lenient treatment or some bond of affection from their masters refer to Negroes from the household staff. Even so, there has been an easy tendency to view this group of slaves in a romantic light, and there is much we really do not know about their life.

A third segment of the slave labor force was composed of skilled and semi-skilled craftsmen. In time Negroes performed substantially all of the work on plantations in certain trades, especially carpentry and cooperage.[36] Frequently, they were also proficient millers, tanners, shoemakers, wheelwrights, spinners, and weavers.[37] Not only did these slave artisans perform tasks necessary for individual plantations; they were also instrumental in the commercial development of the southern colonies, especially in tanning, in the rudimentary iron industry which was developing, and in the preparation of lumber and staves for export.[38]

There are not many extant lists of slaves which provide a specific breakdown of the division of labor on the plantation from which they came. There is one, however, for Green Spring plantation in 1770, when the estate of its deceased owner, Philip Ludwell, was being settled. At that time Ludwell's son-in-law, William Lee, described the slaves at Green Spring as including 59 "crop Negroes," a figure which was "exclusive of boys"; 12 house servants; 4 carpenters; 1 wheelwright; 2 shoemakers, and 3 gardeners and hostlers.[39]

It is easy to overestimate the number of slaves owned by an individual planter and even easier to miscalculate the number

35. *Negro in Virginia*, pp. 35-46, is a general account which leans heavily on a few well-known masters like Jefferson, Wythe, and John Randolph.

36. Jernegan, *Laboring and Dependent Classes*, pp. 9-12.

37. Ibid., pp. 10-12; *Virginia Gazette* (Purdie and Dixon), July 22, 1773; Hening, *Statutes*, 3:403-4.

38. *Virginia Gazette* (Purdie and Dixon), October 31, 1777; Jernegan, *Laboring and Dependent Classes*, pp. 22-23.

39. "Some Notes on 'Green Spring,'" *Virginia Magazine*, 37 (October, 1929): 294.

used to operate a single plantation or quarter. The eighty-odd Negroes at Green Spring were the largest single group from a combined total of 164 on all the lands belonging to Philip Ludwell's estate.[40] This total was more than enough to mark Ludwell as one of the more substantial members of the planter aristocracy, as his membership on the Council also testified.

If we were to judge Ludwell by the pattern of slave ownership revealed in the tax records of the 1780s, he would belong very nearly at the middle of the hundred leading families of the colony. These tax records, which have been most effectively analyzed by Professor Jackson T. Main, furnish the only comprehensive records on how widely slave ownership was distributed in Virginia before the nineteenth century.[41] While the position of the leading families had begun to decline somewhat by the 1780s, the change was as yet so slight that the statistics are generally reliable for the entire later colonial period.[42]

What becomes immediately clear from these tax records is the error of regarding even most of the wealthiest planters as having owned "hundreds" of Negroes. One man, Charles Carter, owned 785. He was followed in turn by William Allen with 700, Robert Beverley of Essex County with 592, Robert Carter of Nomini Hall with 445, and David Ross, the Richmond merchant-planter, with 400. Aside from these top five there were only eighteen other men in the entire colony who owned more than 200 slaves. The average for the hundred leading families was about 180 slaves, eighty on the home plantation and about a hundred elsewhere. A number of families who fell within this top group owned far less than a hundred Negroes.

If there were relatively few large-scale slaveholders in Virginia, the vast majority of families in the average tidewater or piedmont county nonetheless owned at least a small number of Negroes. In a sampling of eight of these counties the records indicated that three-fourths of the heads of families held slaves.

40. Ibid., 293.

41. Jackson T. Main, "The One Hundred," *William and Mary Quarterly*, 3rd ser., 11 (July, 1954): 354-84. Ulrich B. Phillips also used some of these records in *American Negro Slavery* (New York, 1918), pp. 83-84.

42. Main, "One Hundred," pp. 366-67.

Forty per cent of them, however, owned fewer than five Negroes.[43] In the light of these statistics a true picture of slavery in colonial Virginia must take into account the humbler man who owned no more than two or three slaves as well as the more substantial planter.

Until the rationale of the American Revolution had begun to work its logic on the minds of Virginians, any doubt which the average colonist ever had about the wisdom of slavery stemmed either from the unpleasant prospect that the slaves would one day rise up and butcher the master class or else from suspicion that, as a business proposition, slavery simply did not pay its way.[44] The threat of insurrection was in part dealt with through the tightening of the black codes, as well as by the attempt to discourage new importations of Negroes; but it was less easy to deal so directly with the economics of slavery.

The relative advantages and disadvantages of slave labor was, however, a subject often on the mind of the planter. Philip Fithian's account of a conversation with the wife of Robert Carter adequately sums up the reaction in theory of many planters to a situation with which they were unable to deal in fact:

After Supper I had a long conversation with Mrs Carter concerning Negroes in Virginia, & find that She esteems their value at no higher rate than I do. We both concluded, (& I am pretty certain that the conclusion is just) that if in Mr Carters, or in any Gentlemans Estate, all the Negroes should be sold, & the Money put to Interest in safe hands, & let the Lands which these Negroes now work lie wholly uncultivated, the bare Interest of the Price of the Negroes would be a much greater yearly income than what is now received from their working the Lands, making no allowance at all for the trouble & Risk of the Masters as to the Crops, & Negroes.—How much greater then must be the value of an Estate here if these poor enslaved Africans were all in their native desired Country, & in their Room industrious Tenants, who being born in freedom, by a

43. Phillips, *American Negro Slavery,* pp. 83-84.
44. The question of possible moral and humanitarian objections to slavery is treated below, pp. 114-18, 120-26.

laudable care, would not onlyly [sic] inrich their Landlords, but would raise a hardy Offspring to be the Strength & honour of the Colony.[45]

One reason the planters questioned the profit in slave labor was the high cost of investment in slaves. In more pessimistic moments they also criticized their Negroes as wasteful and unproductive workers, either from lack of skill or deliberate resistance to forced labor.[46]

To a large degree, the planters were inclined to rationalize other deficienies in the agricultural methods of the colony at the expense of their Negroes. If there was one way in which slavery succeeded, it was as an economic system. Any problems of debt or credit arising from large investment in slaves was in reality a by-product of the uncertainties of tobacco cultivation. The supposed inefficiency and ineptitude of slave labor was more likely to be the fault of the wasteful methods of farming common to almost everyone who tilled the Virginia soil. Moreover, the cheapness of a slave's maintenance easily outweighed high purchase price, lack of training or skill, and even the prospect of his unproductive old age.[47]

Whatever doubts the Virginia planter may have felt about the wisdom of enslaving an alien people, it must have seemed in the mid-eighteenth century that slavery was certainly here to stay. The rapid growth of the Negro population, the size of the slaveowners' investment, the usefulness of the labor, and outright fear combined to make the replacement of slavery unthinkable.

45. Hunter Dickinson Farish, ed., *Journal and Letters of Philip Vickers Fithian, 1773-1774: A Plantation Tutor of the Old Dominion* (new edn., Williamsburg, Va., 1957), p. 92.

46. "Diary of Col. Landon Carter," *William and Mary Quarterly*, 1st ser., 13 (April, 1905): 223; John Spencer Bassett, ed., *The Writings of "Colonel William Byrd of Westover in Virginia Esqr"* (New York, 1901), pp. 347-48.

47. The most satisfactory discussion of the economic advantages of slavery is Gray, *Agriculture in the Southern United States*, 1: 368-71, 462-80.

CHAPTER III

The Negro in Williamsburg:
An Introduction

FOR AN institution like slavery, which had developed in the first instance out of the needs of an agricultural society, urban life was bound to present something of an anomaly. We know, of course, from the rise of a few sizeable cities in the antebellum South that slavery resolved the contradictions involved with ease. Clearly, however, the use of slaves in a town environment necessitated modifications, if for no other reason than the fact that the largest single element in the slave labor force, the field hands, could have no part in urban slavery. These adjustments were apt to be small in eighteenth-century Virginia, where better than nine-tenths of the population still lived on farms and plantations. But a few towns, Williamsburg among them, had begun to develop as centers of commerce or government.

From the time of its founding Williamsburg was to be linked in many ways with the institution of Negro slavery. The first duty levied by the Assembly against imported Negroes had been intended to furnish money for building the Capitol. And when that construction began one of the first outlays had been £120 to purchase four Negro men "to labor in the business of the capital."[1] Nor should it be forgotten that the founding of Williamsburg came at a time when the institution of slavery had only recently begun to take hardened form in Virginia. Negroes in the colony had been significant in number for barely ten years. True slavery had not existed much longer. The planter class had just begun to appreciate the slaves as a valuable addition to the labor supply of the colony. Williamsburg's development, in short, was to coincide roughly with the real growth of Virginia slavery.

1. *William and Mary Quarterly*, 1st ser., 12 (Oct., 1901): 82.

In a number of ways the story of Williamsburg's Negroes is that of the black population everywhere in the colony. The same laws governed them; the same efforts to evangelize them, by turns fervent and lackadaisical, prevailed; and ultimately the struggle for American independence was to affect them all alike. However, the modifying influence of town life—not only in the different division of labor but also in the relative cosmopolitanism of Williamsburg—had its effect. It was against this background that the Negroes of eighteenth-century Williamsburg lived, providing a minor, but nonetheless important variant on the general history of slavery in Virginia.

CHAPTER IV

Patterns of Slave Population and Ownership in Williamsburg

THE FIRST accurate count of the Negro population of Williamsburg occurs no earlier than in the same tax records of the 1780s that provide the first comprehensive record of the number and distribution of Negroes in all of Virginia. The Williamsburg figures begin with a listing of heads of families in 1782, also used to compute the 1790 United States Census returns for the town. They record a white population of 722 and a Negro population of 702.[1] Over the next few years the total figure for Negroes stayed close to this one: 642 in 1783, 664 in 1784, and 689 in 1786.[2] A few free Negroes counted in 1782 and apparently not added to the later figures account for the small decline. Thus, during the years immediately following the Revolution, the total Negro population remained at about 700. The 50-50 ratio between blacks and whites also continued stable.

After 1786 the tax returns for Williamsburg no longer listed all Negroes but only those 12 years of age or older. Without the younger children it is impossible to determine exactly the total population figure beyond this date; however, we can compare the number of tithable slaves, those over 16, in 1783 with the tithables between 1786 and the end of the century. There were in 1783 a total of 350 tithable Negroes. After 1786 the figure was not much different, ranging between 325 and 353.[3] There is, as a matter of fact, so little variation in the count of tithables that the total Negro population must also have remained very stable. In other words, the Negro population of Williamsburg

1. Evarts B. Greene and Virginia D. Harrington, *American Population Before the Federal Census of 1790* (New York, 1932), p. 153.

2. Williamsburg City. Personal Property Taxes, 1781-1861. Virginia State Library. (Colonial Williamsburg microfilm.)

3. Ibid., 1786-1800. Virginia State Library. (CW microfilm.)

probably stayed at around 700 throughout the last two decades of the century.

Estimating the number of Negroes living in Williamsburg before the Revolution is another matter. There are no tax returns to show either exact population or the ratio of Negroes and whites. The only possible comparison is between a single set of returns of tithables in 1755 and those of 1782-1783;[4] see Table 1. Williamsburg was not listed separately in the 1755 count, however, making it necessary to work with the combined total for James City and York counties and Williamsburg:

TABLE 1
A Comparison of Tithables in 1775 and 1782-1783[5]

	White	Negro	Total	% Negro
	Tithables, 1755			
James City County	394	1254	1648	
York County	562	1567	2129	
Williamsburg	(Included in above figures)			
	956	2821	3777	75%
	Tithables, 1782–83			
James City County	493	1832	2325	
York County	699	2063	2762	
Williamsburg	126	350	476	
	1318	4245	5563	76%

Since Williamsburg cannot be isolated from the total figure, this comparison has its limitations. It at least suggests, however, that the proportion of tithables who were Negro remained about the same, roughly three-quarters. If this ratio remained fixed, then it is not likely that the approximately equal propor-

4. Both male and female Negroes above the age of 16 were counted as tithable, whereas in the white population only males above 21 were counted.

5. Greene and Harrington, *American Population*, pp. 150-53. The James City and York figures are for 1782 and the Williamsburg figures are for 1783.

tion of whites and Negroes in the total population varied significantly either. At any time after the middle of the eighteenth century, then, the Negroes in Williamsburg probably constituted about one-half the total resident population. In this respect Williamsburg did not differ greatly from the rural areas in Tidewater and Piedmont.

There were only a handful of free Negroes counted in Williamsburg in 1782. The four free Negro families listed comprised 11 persons in all, and in each case the head of the family was a woman—Sally Carter, Nanny Jones, Elizabeth Rozario, and Betty Wallace.[6] The voluntary manumission law passed that same year; so the increase in free Negroes resulting from that legislation had not yet begun to occur. To judge from the smallness of the 1782 figure, it is hardly likely that free Negroes were numerous or important in pre-revolutionary Williamsburg.

As in the rest of tidewater and piedmont Virginia, slave holding appears to have been extremely widespread in Williamsburg. Once again it is the tax and census records for the immediate post-revolutionary years that provide the only systematic information about the pattern of slave ownership. Most of the tabulations which follow are drawn from that source.[7] At least five-sixths of families living here in the 1780s owned some slaves, as indicated in Table 2.

TABLE 2

Slave Ownership by Williamsburg Families

Year	Number of Households	Number Owning Slaves	% Owning Slaves
1782	155	135	88%
1783	134	112	84%
1784	112	98	88%

When the number of families owning slaves is compared with the slave population for the same years, the average holding of

6. *First Census of the United States, 1790: Records of the State Enumerations: 1782-1785: Virginia* (Washington, 1908.)

7. Williamsburg City, Personal Property Taxes; *First Census of United States*, Virginia Heads of Families.

an individual family or household works out to five or six Negroes—4.5 per family in 1782, 4.8 in 1783, and 5.9 in 1784. This average figure is not of much value in the sense of enabling one to say that the "typical" Williamsburg family owned exactly 4 or 5 slaves. It is, however, a good indication that extremely large numbers of slaves in a single household were exceptional. There is, however, some indication that this average was increasing, a point which can be amplified from Table 3.

TABLE 3
Size of Slave Holdings of Williamsburg Families

No. of Slaves Owned	Number of Families			Percentage of Families		
	1782	1783	1784	1782	1783	1784
1–2	52	35	20	38.5%	31.2%	20.4%
3–5	38	32	31	28.0%	28.6%	31.6%
6–9	27	27	23	20.0%	21.4%	23.5%
10–19	16	16	22	12.0%	17.9%	22.4%
20 or more	2	2	2	1.5%	0.9%	2.1%
	135	112	98			

Thus, in 1782, more than a third of Williamsburg's slaveowners held no more than one or two Negroes. Then over the next two years the percentage of small owners fell rapidly. Their decline raises the question of whether some of the lesser artisans, journeymen, and other more modest citizens might not have been the first to feel any economic pinch caused by the removal of the capital to Richmond. At any rate there are some 64 heads of families from the 1782 list who do not reappear on subsequent lists, and in almost every case they either owned a small number of slaves or none at all.

Meanwhile the proportion of larger slaveowners increased during these same years (see Table 4), and thereby the total slave population in Williamsburg remained fairly stable. However, the greater number of people continued to keep no more than three to ten slaves; and there were only about two dozen who had more than ten Negroes at any time during this three-year period.

TABLE 4

Williamsburg Residents Owning Ten or More Slaves, 1782-1784

Name	Number of Slaves Listed		
	1782	1783	1784
Robert Anderson	13	12	11
John Blair	18	17	17
Christiana Campbell	19	13	10
Robey Coke	10	2	—
Dudley Digges	—	14	16
James Galt	11	9	8
John Galt	9	10	10
John Greenhow	17	16	20
Corbin Griffin (Sam'l Griffin, 1784)	15	12	13
William Holt	23	21	—
Joseph Hornsby	—	17	10
David Hubard	12	13	—
James Innes	—	9	14
William Lewis	8	8	10
Gabriel Maupin	17	19	17
Elizabeth Nelson	—	—	19
Thomas Nelson	6	—	44
Robert Nicholson	12	12	11
Joseph Prentis	9	11	12
Betty Randolph	15	—	—
George Reid	4	14	13
Mrs. Lewis Riddle	16	15	15
John Saunders	10	11	12
James Southall	21	19	17
Charles Taliaferro	11	13	7
Benjamin Waller	16	13	10
George Wythe	9	14	17

Random examples from the years before 1776 suggest that about the same number of slaves—no more than ten to twenty for even the most prominent citizens—sufficed then as well.[8] The 27 slaves in the inventory of Peyton Randolph's estate in 1776 were the largest number owned by any Williamsburg resident up to that date for which any records could be found.[9] Governor Fauquier owned 17 at his death and John Prentis,

8. See Table No. 5.
9. York County Records, Wills and Inventories, Book 22, pp. 337-41.

who had been mayor of Williamsburg, owned 15.[10] There were many more instances of men who possessed a far smaller number, lending some support to the supposition that the post-revolutionary figures for the percentage of families owning slaves and for the average number of slaves owned by a family were not much different before 1776. See Table 5.

TABLE 5

Examples of Numbers of Slaves Owned in Williamsburg Before 1776

Owner	Year of Death	No. of Slaves in Estate	Ref. in York County Records
John Marot	1717	5	O & W, 15, 242–46
Orlando Jones	1719	10	O & W, 15. 529
David Cunningham	1719	7	O & W, 15, 562
Robert Davidson	1739	3	W & I, 18. 587–88
John Carter	1741	4	W & I, 19. 91–92
Thomas Pattison	1742	6	W & I. 19, 177–79
William Keith	?	8	W & I, 19, 282
John Burdett	1746	6	W & I, 20, 46–48
Ishmael Moody	1748	10	W & I, 20, 134–38
James Wray	1750	20	W & I, 20, 204–08
Mark Cosby	1752	5	W & I, 20, 277
Kenneth MacKenzie	1755	5	W & I, 20, 364–66
Henry Weatherburn	1760	13	W & I, 21, 43
John Coke	1768	9	W & I, 21, 381–84
Peter Hay	1769	11	W & I, 21, 444–48
William Waters	1769	6	W & I, 21, 463-66
Anthony Hay	1771	20	W & I, 22, 19–24
Francis Fauquier	1771	17	W & I, 22, 91ff.
Joseph Scrivener	1772	4	W & I, 22, 118–120
Thomas Cobb	1774	4	W & I, 22, 245–46
Matthew Tuell	1775	2	W & I, 22, 253–54
Matthew Moody	1775	4	W & I, 22, 296–97
John Prentis	1775	15	W & I, 22, 313–20
Alexander Craig	1776	8	W & I, 22, 330–37
Peyton Randolph	1776	27	W & I, 22, 337–41
Alexander Purdie	1779	13	W & I, 22, 437–42
Henry Bowcock	1779	5	W & I, 22, 447–48

In the final analysis four major conclusions stand out about the slave population and the pattern of slave ownership in

10. Ibid., pp. 313-20.

Williamsburg during the immediate post-revolutionary years. And, in a much more tentative way, they can also be applied to the more flourishing years before the removal of the seat of government. They are:

1. The number of Negroes and whites in the resident population of Williamsburg was approximately equal.

2. An overwhelming majority, roughly five-sixths, of the families in Williamsburg owned slaves.

3. A large percentage of these slaveowners were, nevertheless, persons of modest estate who might own no more than one or two slaves. After the Revolution, however, the proportion of small-scale owners was decreasing rapidly.

4. Even the wealthier men, innkeepers, etc., who were among the larger slaveowners in Williamsburg, normally kept only a moderate number of slaves, usually from about ten to fifteen and seldom more than twenty.

CHAPTER V

The Work of the Negro
in Williamsburg

To MAKE too much of eighteenth-century Williamsburg as an urban economy may be inaccurate to a degree, since the Virginia capital owed its creation and its continuing life so largely to the business of politics and government. To a large extent the town represented a concentration of semi-agrarian households whose gardens provided much of the food for both local residents and visitors. Operating plantations, moreover, extended to the town limits. Still, there were enough features of genuine town life—the presence of a number of merchants and craftsmen, the crowded public times, etc.—to insure that the economic function of Williamsburg's slaves was distinctive from that of the plantation Negroes.

Of all the impressions which one forms from reading through the newspaper advertisements that are the chief source of information about slave occupations in Williamsburg, the one which stands out most strongly is that of a preponderance of "domestic Negroes," slaves who were engaged in all the usual tasks of running a household. Advertisements for the sales of lots of Negroes were likely to specify that they were "valuable Slaves, chiefly House Servants" or "valuable Slaves, being the servants usually employed in and about the house and kitchen."[1] Where listings of such slaves stated the skills and occupations of each, various domestic servants—cooks, waiters, slaves accustomed to general house work, etc.—predominated. There is a measure of statistical evidence for the large number of domestic slaves. In a group of 104 Negroes chosen at random from among those sold in Williamsburg at various times, advertisements for the sale of 60 give information about their previous work. Out of the 60 a total of 47 had been domestic

1. *Virginia Gazette* (Dixon and Hunter), December 23, 1775; (Purdie and Dixon), April 5, 1770.

servants of one type or another as against 13 craftsmen. This is not a large sampling, but it is at least a clue to the proportion of household slaves in the general slave population.

Many of the slaves, both male and female, used for domestic work were simply general house workers—"House Wench" was the most frequent term used to describe the women so employed. For example, among the 47 household slaves tabulated above, 23 were advertised as experienced in general house work. This did not necessarily mean that they were the least skilled domestics. A good "house wench" could often perform any number of tasks, such as the one who understood "cooking, making paste, pickling, washing, ironing, cleaning house, and spinning."[2] Another was "well qualified for all Sorts of House-work, as Washing, Ironing, Sewing. Brewing, Baking &c."[3] A Negro boy of 18 whom Robert Nicolson advertised for sale in 1778 had been "used to the house ever since a child" and was especially good at cleaning or waiting table.[4]

There were, however, other house slaves trained for one or two specific duties. Logically only a relatively well-to-do owner would have the necessary hands to divide household labors too minutely. Where any degree of specialization occurred, it was usually the cook whose work was first separated from general household duties. Probably personal menservants were next in frequency. After that the division of labor might be made in a number of ways with slaves assigned especially to the laundry, the garden, or the stables. It is surprising that in the entire group of advertisements relating to Williamsburg slaves no reference occurs to Negro women trained as personal maids for the ladies of the household. Below are the specific occupations that are mentioned at one time or another:

Nurse	Gardener
Washer and Ironer	Coachman
Cook	Hostler
Seamstress	Personal Manservant
Spinner	Waiter
Butcher	

2. Ibid., (Rind), September 26, 1771.
3. Ibid., June 6, 1745.
4. Ibid., (Purdie), March 20, 1778.

Something has already been said of the abilities of many slaves who were listed simply as general houseworkers. The Negroes who performed more specialized jobs were in many cases no less skilled. Phrases such as "exceeding good Washer and Ironer" or "exceeding fine cook" occur frequently. To some degree these claims may be of a piece with the twentieth-century used-car dealer's extravagant advertisements of his wares; but some of the descriptions are almost too detailed to be completely discredited. There was, for example, one young mulatto woman, an experienced spinner and knitter, whom her master claimed could "cut out and make up linen as well as any servant in *Virginia*."[5] Others were well trained in two or more types of work—a mulatto of 17 who was both a waiter and a hairdresser; a Negro man of 25 trained as a hostler, gardener, and house servant; or another man who has waited on gentlemen but was also a tailor.[6]

Occasionally personal and household slaves of really unusual qualifications turned up for sale in Williamsburg. Sukey Hamilton, who had been Governor Fauquier's cook before his death, was offered at public sale on December 15, 1768.[7] Probably no slave could have offered a wider range of qualifications than one who was offered for sale as:

A very valuable young Negro man, who understands cleaning of a house, and is well qualified to wait on a single Gentleman, or a family, a very good gardener, and a tolerable good cook, butcher, and plaisterer, and in short very handy at anything. He is also sober, very honest, and can play on the violin.[8]

The most remarkable of all, however, was:

A Valuable young handsome Negro Fellow, about 18 or 20 years of age, has every qualification of a genteel and sensible

5. Ibid., (Purdie), October 25, 1776.
6. Ibid., (Purdie and Dixon), July 11, 1773; (Dixon and Hunter), March 30, 1776; (Purdie), June 7, 1776.
7. Ibid., (Purdie and Dixon), November 24, 1768. The Rev. James Horrocks had purchased her from the Fauquier estate at a relatively high price, and presumably it was he who then sold her again in 1768, for reasons not known. York County Records, Wills and Inventories, Book 22, p. 91ff.
8. *Virginia Gazette* (Rind), October 19, 1769.

servant, and has been in many different parts of the world. He shaves, dresses hair, and plays on the *French* horn. He lately came from *London*, and has with him two suits of new clothes, and his *French* horn, which the purchaser may have with him.[9]

A governor's cook, a man with a half dozen talents, or a world-traveled slave are admittedly well beyond the ordinary. However, even the more conventional descriptions imply a high level of skill and experience. With due allowance for the fact that most of these words of praise come from advertisements, the impression still remains that the domestic slaves of Williamsburg represented as able and well-trained a group of Negroes as lived anywhere in the colony.

Statistics in the preceding chapter indicated that easily five-sixths of the families in Williamsburg owned at least a single slave. With slaveholding so common, few households can have been without some domestic help. Nor can the possession of a few slaves to perform the house work have been much of a mark of social distinction in eighteenth-century Williamsburg. There must have been many modest homes in which one or two Negroes labored at every task from cooking and cleaning to gardening.

Even in the case of more prosperous citizens of Williamsburg, the number of slaves needed to maintain their households does not seem to have been excessively large. This is borne out by the fact that these men usually owned no more than ten to twenty slaves. George Wythe and Benjamin Waller, for example, held 14 and 13 respectively in 1783.[10] Francis Fauquier had evidently met the social demands of the governorship with a staff of 17 slaves, and five of these were small children.[11]

The comparatively large number of inns and ordinaries required for the busy public seasons of Williamsburg added a significant number of slaves trained for house work to the town's Negro population. Many of the inns appear to have

9. Ibid., (Purdie and Dixon), July 23, 1767.
10. Williamsburg City, Personal Property Taxes, 1783.
11. York County Records, Wills and Inventories, Book 22, p. 91.

operated much as any large household with about the same number of slaves and something of the same distribution of work. Anthony Hay, one of the keepers of the Raleigh, owned 20 slaves at the time of his death in early 1771.[12] When his estate was sold in March of that year, nineteen of the slaves, including "a very good Cabinet Maker, a good Coachman and Carter, some fine Waiting Boys, good Cooks, Washers, &c.," were offered for sale.[13] There are some other examples of innkeepers with roughly the same number of slaves: Henry Wetherburn, for instance, with an inventory of 13 in 1760 and James Southall with about 20 in the years just after the Revolution.[14] Many keepers of smaller establishments operated with a more limited number of slaves. One early innkeeper, Thomas Pattison, left an estate in 1742 that included six slaves, two of them small children.[15] John Burdett, who left six slaves in 1746; Henry Bowcock, five in 1779; and Richard Charlton, seven in 1780 were similar cases.[16]

The level of service that the slaves of Williamsburg's innkeepers provided may not have been uniformly good, but at least one traveler found it highly satisfactory:

In our hotel we had a very good though dear entertainment, Negro cooks, women waiters, and chambermaids made their courtesies with a great deal of native grace and simple elegance and were dressed neatly and cleanly. They yet recall and speak with evident delight of the politeness and gallantry of the French officers.[17]

A number of Negroes were also employed for various housekeeping tasks at the College of William and Mary, apparently

12. Ibid., pp. 19-24.
13. *Virginia Gazette* (Purdie and Dixon), January 17, 1771.
14. York County Records, Wills and Inventories, Book 21, p. 43; Williamsburg City, Personal Property Taxes, 1783-84.
15. York County Records, Wills and Inventories, Book 19, pp. 177-79.
16. Ibid., Book 20, pp. 46-48; Book 22, pp. 447-48, 469-70.
17. "A Journey from Philadelphia to Charleston, 1783." Virginia State Library, quoted in Raymond B. Pinchbeck, "The Virginia Negro Artisan and Tradesman," *Publications of the University of Virginia*, Phelps-Stokes Fellowship Papers, No. 7 (Richmond, Va., 1926), p. 39.

from a very early date. It was a Negro man who went with Commissary Blair to force the doors of the grammar school in the celebrated "barring out" incident of 1702 and Governor Nicholson gave the college a Negro man valued at £30 in 1704.[18] In addition to its slaves in Williamsburg, the college also owned Negroes on its lands along the Nottoway River.[19] Students also occasionally brought personal servants with them to Williamsburg. In 1754 there were eight slave boys at William and Mary, brought to wait on their young masters.[20]

Generally the college's Negroes at Williamsburg worked under the direction of the housekeeper. One housekeeper, whose supervision was not all that the president and masters wished, was ordered in 1763 not to trust the Negroes with keys or to go away from the college too often, "As we all know that Negroes will not perform their Duties without the Mistress's constant Eye especially in so large a Family as the College."[21]

It is not clear how many Negroes were normally used at the college, but in 1768 it was necessary to hire two extra ones for cutting and carting wood.[22] Three years later the college officials planned to purchase a Negro woman from Lord Botetourt's estate for college use.[23] It may have been more or less a regular practice to use some hired Negroes, because in the fall of 1777, when the president and masters decided to sell the land on the Nottoway and the slaves held there, they planned to bring two men and a boy from there to replace hired Negroes at Williamsburg.[24]

More elaborate changes occurred in December, 1779, as a result of the discontinuance of the grammar school and the commons. The kitchen Negroes were to be leased to a steward who would contract to provide meals for students, a sufficient number of slaves were to be retained for cleaning, and any

18. "William and Mary College Historical Notes," Manuscript Report, Colonial Williamsburg Research Dept., pp. 95, 96, 99, 145.

19. Ibid., p. 235.

20. *William and Mary Quarterly*, 1st ser., 6 (January, 1898): 187-88.

21. Journal of Meetings of President and Masters, College of William and Mary, pp. 109-11.

22. Ibid., p. 167.

23. "William and Mary College Historical Notes," p. 202.

24. Journal of Meetings of Presidents and Masters, pp. 269-70.

surplus ones were to be hired out at public auction.[25] It turned out that the steward was allowed two men and a boy and that five slaves were retained for cleaning.[26] Then in 1782 some of these remaining eight or else some of the ones offered for lease were to be sold to meet the cost of repairing the buildings.[27]

Predominant as the slaves engaged in domestic work were in the Negro population of Williamsburg, they did not entirely overshadow a smaller group of skilled and semiskilled slave craftsmen. Such slaves appeared fairly frequently for sale here. Occasionally lots of Negroes were simply advertised as having "among them some good Tradesmen."[28] But more often than not skilled craftsmen would be sold individually or singled out for special mention in an advertisement of a larger group of Negroes—an indication of a ready market for them. The demand, in fact, was great enough for the leasing of Negro artisans to become a profitable operation.[29]

In many cases slaves may have received such training as they had in a craft by the most informal sort of apprenticeship, perhaps working alongside some Negro craftsman and eventually absorbing whatever skill the older slave possessed. But it was also customary to bind slaves for a term of apprenticeship under a free craftsman.[30] Matthew Tuell, a carpenter living near town on Capitol Landing Road, had apprenticed to him in 1772 two Negro boys belonging to William Digges, Jr., of Yorktown.[31] In another instance, an unidentified purchaser sought to buy two other Negro boys for the specific purpose of apprenticing them in some trade.[32]

Carpentry was rather clearly the most frequently practiced trade among Williamsburg's Negro artisans, as was also the

25. *Virginia Gazette* (Dixon and Nicolson), December 18, 1779.
26. Journal of Meetings of President and Masters, p. 280.
27. Ibid., pp. 295-96.
28. *Virginia Gazette* (Purdie and Dixon), April 11, 1771.
29. Ibid., September 12, 1745; (Purdie), November 24, 1775; January 10, 1777; December 5, 1777; December 12, 1777; January 19, 1778; March 27, 1778; (Dixon and Nicolson), July 24, 1779.
30. Pinchbeck, "Negro Artisan," pp. 29-30.
31. *Virginia Gazette* (Purdie and Dixon), June 11, 1772.
32. Ibid., (Dixon and Hunter), September 7, 1776.

case among plantation craftsmen throughout Virginia.[33] Shoe-makers and blacksmiths were the next most often represented. There were, besides these three, at least an occasional slave trained in several other trades. Recorded evidence exists that the following crafts at one time or another were followed by slaves in Williamsburg:

Barber	Cooper
Blacksmith	Crafter
Butcher	Harnessmaker
Cabinetmaker	Shoemaker
Carpenter and joiner	Tanner
Carter	Tailor

Much of the information about Negro craftsmen in Williamsburg accords with a general pattern throughout the southern colonies. Nevertheless, there are strong suggestions that neither the actual number of Negro artisans in the Virginia capital nor the range of crafts in which they were experienced was as large as elsewhere.

It has become a widely accepted view that such slaves became so numerous in many trades that white craftsmen in the South all but disappeared through emigration or change of occupation. In Charleston, where slaves became proficient in every craft including even that of jeweler, the white artisan class was virtually eliminated by 1790.[34] The same thing has been described as happening in Virginia, and it may well have on most plantations.[35] However, no suggestion of competition between white and Negro craftsmen in Williamsburg has as yet been found. No reference exists to laws here, as there were in South Carolina, that limited the number of Negro apprentices.[36] So far as we know, in the years in which Williamsburg flourished as the capital its white craftsmen remained a vigorous,

33. Pinchbeck, "Negro Artisan," p. 32, for Virginia. The evidence of carpentry as the leading trade among Williamsburg slaves rests on its more frequent mention in issues of the *Virginia Gazette.*

34. Leila Sellers, *Charleston Business on the Eve of the American Revolution* (Chapel Hill, N.C., 1934), pp. 102-5.

35. Pinchbeck, "Negro Artisan," pp. 25-26.

36. Sellers, *Charleston Business,* pp. 102-5.

flourishing group. Even as late as the 1780s, about thirty-seven remained.[37]

There is, of course, the possibility that competition between slave and free craftsmen might have been eliminated, if a situation prevailed in which the white artisans owned and employed Negroes skilled in the same trade. One or two fairly clear examples of an operation of this sort in Williamsburg do exist. During the early years of the Revolution a carpenter and joiner named Francis Jaram employed a number of helpers, some of them slaves. He advertised at least twice in 1777 for sizeable numbers of house carpenters and Negro carpenters.[38] He leased some of the Negroes; but others were his own property. Jaram's slaves included a Negro carpenter named Harry, advertised as a runaway in the spring of 1777 about the time his master was trying to acquire the additional slaves.[39] An interesting detail about Harry was his master's observation that "when he works at a Bench he works on the wrong Side." There was also in Williamsburg a tan works, operated by William Pearson and employing four slaves who were experienced tanners and curriers, two shoemakers, and a carpenter.[40]

Jaram's and Pearson's methods, however, may be isolated examples. The average craftsman, it is true, seemed likely to own a few more slaves than the general run of Williamsburg slaveholders. A few examples include Alexander Purdie, the printer, who owned 13 at the time of his death; James Wray, a carpenter, with 20; Humphrey Harwood, a mason, with 10; and Peter Hay, an apothecary, with 11.[41] It turns out, however, in a number of instances that relatively few of their Negroes were adult males. And of those who were adult males, few have a high enough valuation in the inventory of the estate to make it appear that they were trained in their master's craft. Table 6 provides some illustrations of this point. The large proportion of

37. *First Census of the United States . . . Virginia.*
38. *Virginia Gazette* (Dixon and Hunter), March 21, 1777; (Purdie), July 25, 1777.
39. Ibid., (Dixon and Hunter), April 25, 1777.
40. Ibid., (Dixon and Hunter), March 7, 1777.
41. The inventory of Harwood's estate is in York County Records, Wills and Inventories, Book 23, pp. 219-20. For the others, see below, Table No. 6.

TABLE 6

Adult Male Slaves of High Valuation in the Estates of Williamsburg Craftsmen

Reference in York County Records	Craftsman—	Craft	Year	Total Slaves	Adult Males	Males, High Valuation
W & I, Bk. 22, 330–37	Alexander Craig	Saddler	1776	8	1	1
O & W, Bk. 15, 562	David Cunningham	Barber	1719	7	1	0
W & I, Bk. 18, 587–88	Robert Davidson	Physician	1739	3	1	0
W & I, Bk. 23, 1–2	Cornelius Deforest	Baker	1782	6	4	1
W & I, Bk. 21, 444–48	Peter Hay	Apothecary	1769	11	1	1
W & I, Bk. 20, 364–66	Kenneth Mackenzie	Apothecary	1755	5	0	0
W & I, Bk. 22, 296–97	Matthew Moody	Cabinetmaker	1775	4	1	1
W & I, Bk. 22, 437–42	Alexander Purdie	Printer	1779	13	3(?)	2
W & I Bk. 20, 204–08	James Wray	Carpenter	1750	20	7(?)	3
				72	18	9

female slaves and children, the small number of males, and the even smaller number of really valuable males suggest that the slaves belonging to craftsmen, much like those of other Williamsburg residents, were largely domestics. There is some additional support for this supposition in the compilation of *Virginia Gazette* advertisements already discussed above. There, it will be remembered, the Negroes identified as craftsmen numbered only about a fourth as many as those known to be household servants, 13 out of a total of 104 to be exact.

Moreover, the dozen or so crafts in which Williamsburg's Negroes are definitely known to have been employed as small in comparison with those in which slaves elsewhere in Virginia and in the other colonies engaged. Easily fifty different skilled occupations of Virginia plantation Negroes can be counted from the *Virginia Gazette*.[42]

There are few indications of the level of ability of the slave artisans who worked in Williamsburg. Occasionally there is a reference to an exceptionally skilled Negro. William Trebell, who lived near Williamsburg, owned a 26-year old slave, Bob, who was described in the following terms: "He is an extraordinary sower, a tolerable good carpenter and currier, pretends to make shoes, and is a very good tailor."[43] Lewis, a youth of only 18 or 19, belonging to Richard Wynne from near Yorktown, was an accomplished shoemaker.[44] Both these slaves were runaways, and both were successful in passing themselves off as free men. Lewis had called himself Lewis Roberts and remained as close to home as Williamsburg.

There is a suggestion in the use of the term "Negro carpenter" that Negro artisans were not always so skilled. As employed, it seems to denote not just a slave who happened to be a carpenter but a worker whose abilities were less than those of a white artisan. Francis Jaram, for instance, had sought in the same advertisement to hire "good house carpenters" and "Negro carpenters."[45] One suspects there is a precise distinction

42. Lester J. Cappon and Stella F. Duff, eds., *Virginia Gazette Index, 1736-1780* (Williamsburg, Va., 1950), 2:1076-80.
43. *Virginia Gazette* (Purdie and Dixon), April 16, 1767.
44. Ibid., (Dixon and Hunter), July 10, 1778.
45. Ibid., (Dixon and Hunter), March 21, 1777.

here that would have been quite clear to those who read his announcement. Other advertisements employed the same term or spoke of a slave as being a "tolerable good carpenter."[46] It may well have been that most of the slave carpenters here—and they were the most numerous of the Negro artisans—were more nearly semi-skilled than skilled laborers.

Slave labor was also employed in two relatively large-scale undertakings in Williamsburg which went beyond the usual craft operation. The first of these was the vinyard established by public authority under the direction of a French winemaker, Andrew Estave.[47] It included a tract of about 200 acres located a mile and half outside town. Negro slaves were purchased with public funds to cultivate the vines, and through the years of actual operation Estave seemed to have an unusual amount of difficulty with runaways.[48] Then in March, 1777, both the land and the slaves were put up for sale.

The disruption of trade during the American Revolution resulted in the establishment of the Manufacturing Society of Williamsburg, in effect a small factory utilizing slave labor. In the fall of 1776 it prepared to undertake the weaving of cloth, advertising for a superintendent and some spinners and weavers.[49] The following February the society sought a number of slaves and also indicated it would accept Negro girls as apprentices.[50] The Negroes that the society wanted to purchase included five or six Negro boys from 15 to 20 years of age, a similar number of girls from 12 to 15, and one or two weavers. The slaves employed at the Manufactory, as it came to be called, were soon producing some quantity of fabric, as four hundred yards of "hempen linen" plus a piece of imitation corduroy were offered for sale in the summer of 1777.[51]

It fell to the lot of the Negro in Williamsburg, as everywhere

46. Ibid., (Purdie and Dixon), November 4, 1773; (Purdie), September 6, 1776.

47. Ibid., (Purdie), February 28, 1777.

48. Ibid., (Purdie and Dixon), October 22, 1772; November 18, 1773; March 24, 1774; (Pinkney), October 13, 1774; (Dixon and Hunter), March 23, 1776.

49. Ibid., (Purdie), September 6, 1776.

50. Ibid., (Dixon and Hunter), February 7, 1777.

51. Ibid., (Purdie), July 25, 1777.

else, to perform the most difficult or the most menial tasks. In town, where the slave was spared the more demanding labor in the fields, his normal duties as a household servant or as an artisan may seem a light burden. Still, it would be a mistake to underestimate the endless amount of drudgery required to make an eighteenth-century household function. The slaves here in Williamsburg, however, proved themselves capable of developing a high level of ability. This applied especially to the best of the household slaves, although there were examples of skilled Negro craftsmen.

In the light of the wide employment of Negro artisans throughout the southern colonies, the degree to which household servants seem to outnumber craftsmen in Williamsburg is surprising. One result of this was to reduce the importance of the slaves as a factor in the economic life of Williamsburg. Their function was primarily one of personal service. For this very reason, however, no representation of the everyday life and work of Williamsburg would be completely accurate if it did not depict the slaves engaged in their daily round of household duties.

CHAPTER VI

The Auction Block:
Williamsburg As a Slave Market

N O SINGLE feature of slavery arouses more unpleasant reactions than the buying and selling of men and women, as if they were so many livestock. The auction block was, however, an inescapable consequence of having slavery at all; and Williamsburg could hardly be free of this aspect of slave life. The capital had its favorite spots for public sales, and few weeks went by in which there was not some trading in Negroes.

A large proportion of the advertised sales of slaves in Williamsburg were simply casual offers to dispose of a single Negro, or, at the most, two or three. Forerunners of the present-day classified advertisements, the listings of these slaves in the *Virginia Gazette* soon fell into a stereotyped format.[1] Usually such notices did not identify the seller, and they almost never indicated either the price or reason for selling.[2] There would simply be a brief description of the Negro involved, and the interested purchaser was expected to "apply to the Printer" for details. The actual sale in these cases was presumably negotiated privately between owner and buyer without resort to public auction. It seems that such sales would almost certainly have involved only individual slave owners who for any number of reasons—a pressing debt, for example—may have found it necessary to dispose of a Negro or two. Such transactions can hardly have had any great commercial significance.

A far greater number of Negroes changed hands, however, at public sales which occurred with great frequency in

1. See, for example, *Virginia Gazette* (Purdie and Dixon), September 29, 1774; (Dixon and Hunter), January 28, 1775; (Purdie), March 8, 1776; (Dixon and Hunter), August 24, 1776.

2. One of the few advertisements to include an asking price was inserted by Robert Nicolson in the *Virginia Gazette* (Purdie), for March 20, 1778. Nicolson asked £ 150 sterling for a Negro boy of 18 who was an experienced house servant.

Williamsburg. While there were a number of occasions for these auctions, they almost all shared the fact that they were actions at law. The most common purpose, for instance, was to settle the estate of a deceased resident. In just over half the cases in which the occasion for a sale is specified, the slaves up for auction were part of an estate. Sometimes they were offered along with the rest of the personal property of the deceased and at other times were held for separate sale.

Most of the remaining public sales of Negroes were held to settle judgments of the courts, most often of the county court for James City. Occasionally there was also a sale held on order of the York County Court.[3] In a few cases the General Court as well ordered the Negroes sold:

By virtue of a decree of the Hon. the General Court, obtained by Mess. *Capel* and *Osgood Hanbury*, of *London*, against Col. *Philip Rootes*, will be sold, for *ready money*, before Mr. *Hay's* door, in *Williamsburg*, the 16th of this instant (June) eight valuable NEGROES.[4]

Like Col. Rootes's slaves, many of the Negroes involved in these court sales had been seized to pay their masters' debts.

New occasions for the selling of slaves by legal directive arose during the Revolution, when it is possible to find slaves, the late property of a fleeing Loyalist, being advertised for auction on the order of the Committee of Safety.[5] Nor did the Patriots overlook Lord Dunmore whose Negroes and personal estate were sold at the Palace.[6]

Except for a few instances in which persons leaving Virginia to return to England or to move elsewhere advertised their slaves, one or the other of the above legal actions were the only reasons ever advanced for various public auctions in Williamsburg.[7] There were, of course, sales from time to time

3. Ibid., (Purdie and Dixon), September 22, 1768.
4. Ibid., (Purdie and Dixon), June 8, 1769.
5. Ibid., (Purdie), June 7, 1776.
6. Ibid., (Dixon and Hunter), June 22, 1776.
7. In 40 *Virginia Gazette* advertisements, in which the occasion for a sale of slaves is explained, 23 such sales were settlements of estates, 13 were settlements of judgments of the courts, and 4 were sales of the property of persons leaving the colony.

for which no explanation was offered. But the typical public auction of slaves in Williamsburg was likely to be an executor's or a sheriff's sale.

Though the Market Square might have seemed a logical choice, there was no established slave market in colonial Williamsburg. By the nineteenth century an auction block stood on the Court House Green; and the auctioneer's cry, "Here they go," could regularly be heard there.[8] But in the eighteenth century far and away the favored location was the front of the Raleigh Tavern, one more indication of the Raleigh's pre-eminence as a busy center of Williamsburg life. Once in a while another tavern served—Gabriel Maupin's, Trebell's, or some other.[9] A few sales also took place at the James City County Court House.[10] Sometimes the public sale of an estate was held at the home of the deceased, since the house itself and the furnishings might also be up for sale. Executors just as frequently, however, had the slaves and other portions of the estate auctioned at the Raleigh. All in all, the Raleigh had an unrivalled position as the customary slave market for Williamsburg all through the eighteenth century.[11]

There would seem to have been financial advantages in fixing the date of a sale of slaves during meetings of the General Court whenever possible. Nevertheless, there is no clear evidence that these crowded occasions were particularly favored. In two recorded instances sales were, however, advertised to take place during the Meeting of the Merchants,[12] but in one case several slaves experienced in handling river craft were offered and in the other, a serving boy being brought down

8. Eliza Baker, "Memoirs of Williamsburg, Virginia," Typescript of conversation between Eliza Baker, an ex-slave, and W. A. R. Goodwin, May 4, 1933, in Colonial Williamsburg Archives, p. 5.

9. *Virginia Gazette,* October 17, 1752; (Purdie and Dixon), December 4, 1766; (Dixon and Hunter). February 25, 1775.

10. Ibid., (Rind), June 29, 1769; (Pinkney), December 29, 1774; (Purdie), January 24, 1777.

11. Of 62 sales in which the location is specified 37 took place at the Raleigh, 14 at private homes, 5 at other taverns, and 4 at the James City County Courthouse.

12. Ibid., (Purdie and Dixon), October 28, 1773; October 20, 1774.

from Tappahannock by a merchant. So these were both sales of special interest to the merchants. There were also some auctions during oyer and terminer court sessions.[13] But for the most part, if Negroes were to be sold on a court day, it was more likely to be a meeting of one of the local courts, probably the James City county court.[14]

One of the most difficult things of all to determine is the price which Negroes generally brought in Williamsburg, since it was not customary to give a price wanted in advertising Negroes for sale in the *Gazette* and since nothing survives in the way of records of the level of prices at auctions. William Campbell, a militia officer from western Virginia, complained of the prices around Williamsburg in early 1776: "Negroes are exceeding dear in this part of the Country; 100 pounds and from that to 130 or 140 is given for Negroe wenches; indeed I think they can be bought much cheaper in any of the back Counties than here—"[15]

Prices had, by the time Campbell wrote, already begun the inflationary spiral of the revolutionary years. They continued to climb in terms of current money to the point that assessors of estates in Williamsburg by 1779 valued the average adult male slave at a figure of around £1000.[16] In the more stable situation which prevailed before the Revolution a good male slave in Virginia is supposed to have brought about £28 to £35 sterling in the first half of the eighteenth century and about £40 sterling after mid-century.[17] The assessments for inventories of estates in Williamsburg indicate a slightly steadier rise:[18]

These valuations from inventories of estates are, of course,

13. Ibid., May 12, 1738; October 15, 1752.

14. Ibid., (Purdie and Dixon), June 18, 1767; July 25, 1771; (Rind), June 29, 1769; (Purdie), January 24, 1777.

15. January 15, 1776, Campbell-Preston Papers, Manuscripts Division, Library of Congress (Colonial Williamsburg microfilm), I-60.

16. York County Records, Wills and Inventories, Book 22, pp. 437-42.

17. Elizabeth Donnan, ed., *Documents Illustrative of the Slave Trade to America* (Washington, 1935), 4:6-7.

18. These estimates are based on a comparison of the inventories of Williamsburg estates available in the York County Records.

Year	Estimated Average Value of Adult Male Slaves
1740's	£40
1750's	£50–£60
1770–1771	£60–£75
1775	£100

estimates; and it would be helpful to know whether the public sales of the Negroes so inventoried brought in less or more money. The one estate for which there seems to be such a record is that of Governor Fauquier, and in every case his slaves sold for less than the amount for which they were listed in the inventory:[19]

Slaves	Value in Inventory	Purchase Price	Purchaser
John[20]	£ 40	£ 30	Thomas Everard
Bristol	55	41	Thomas Everard
Sukey and 2 children	140	105	Jas. Horrocks
Lancaster	70	52.10	Chris. Ayscough
Tidus	55	41.5	R. C. Nicholas
Tom		45	John Dixon
Mary and 1 child	70	52.10	John Dixon
John, Sall and 2 children	130	104	Geo. Gilmer
Moll	40	30	Richard Johnson
Nanny and 1 child (child died and discount allowed in purchase)	65	41.5	James Geddy

The clearest impression that emerges from what is known about the buying and selling of slaves in Williamsburg is that the town was never in the colonial period a slave market of any size or commercial importance. The sales that went on here, frequent as they were, turned out to be almost exclusively legal

19. York County Records, Wills and Inventories, Book 22, p. 91ff. Fauquier had moreover specified that the slaves should, where possible, go at less than the market value to the master of their own choice.

20. There are both a Young John and an Old John in the inventory with valuations of £60 and £40 respectively. The relative sale prices suggest that Everard purchased Old John.

rather than economic in motive. To be sure, the sellers intended to realize as much of a financial return as possible; but the sale arose in the first place out of some legal necessity—an estate to be settled, a debt to be discharged by court order, or something similar.

Commercial traffic in slaves in the eighteenth century usually suggested first of all the slave ship landing its cargo of raw Negroes direct from some spot on the African coast. Trade in imported slaves also included Negroes from the West Indies who came in smaller numbers, though in more frequent shipments.[21] This entire foreign commerce in slaves was one in which Williamsburg did not seem to figure. The Naval Office for the Upper James was located here so that cargoes of Negroes which were to be sold in that customs district should have been registered in Williamsburg.[22] But there is no existing record of recently imported Negroes being sold here as they were at Yorktown and at nearby points on the James.[23] In fact, many of the advertisements of Negroes offered for sale in Williamsburg make a particular point of emphasizing that they were "Virginia born," the expectation being that Negroes born in the colonies were better trained and more valuable.[24]

There were still other characteristics which made the market in slaves in the capital almost certainly a local one. County court days were more popular as the date of a sale than the times when the General Court was sitting. The slaves auctioned here seem to have nearly all been locally owned. In only a few cases did they come from any distance. There are the two instances in which slaves were brought in to be sold at the

21. Donnan, *Documents*, 4: 183-234.

22. Two ships, the *Rae Galley* and the *Lilly*, were seized and condemned by an Admiralty Court in Williamsburg on October 5, 1769, for failure to register their cargoes of slaves with the collector. They were sold, however, at Martin's Brandon. *Virginia Gazette* (Rind), October 5, 1769.

23. See, for example, *Virginia Gazette*, August 9, 1736; June 8, 1739; and October 27, 1752, for Yorktown. For Bermuda Hundred on the James, see, ibid., (Purdie and Dixon), September 5, 1766; August 11, 1768; May 18, 1769.

24. Ibid., October 17, 1752; (Purdie and Dixon), December 18, 1766; March 31, 1768.

Meeting of the Merchants.[25] Then in 1773 the sheriff of Middlesex County delivered "A Large Parcel of Young Virginia born Slaves" to Williamsburg for sale at the Raleigh on April 30.[26] Perhaps Williamsburg prices were already so notoriously high that Middlesex decided to capitalize on the situation. But with the evidence now available, this stands as an isolated case.

A final argument against any large-scale commercial dealing in slaves in Williamsburg is the small number of Negroes involved in the average public sale. Quite commonly there would be only a single Negro to be auctioned; and in many other cases only two or three were sold at one time. Out of a total of 76 advertised sales, in which the number of slaves to be offered is definitely stated, 8 listed between 10 and 20 slaves; 6 listed 20 to 30; and only 2 mentioned a larger number. The two largest were each auctions of about 50 slaves, which is a sizeable enough number to raise the possibility that a merchant might have been involved. One of these sales, however, was a York County sheriff's sale of "About fifty choice slaves, men, women, boys, and girls; belonging to *Armistead Lightfoot,* and taken in execution to satisfy several judgments of *York* court."[27] There simply was not in Williamsburg enough trading in slaves on a scale large enough to interest the merchants of the colony.[28]

There is a certain contradiction in emphasizing how frequent and commonplace the public auction of slaves must have been in Williamsburg and then saying that so brisk a market in Negroes was really lacking in economic significance. Yet no other summarization of what we know about the buying and selling of slaves in Williamsburg fits the available evidence. The citizen of Williamsburg who found himself in need of an additional servant or two did not turn to the captain who advertised that he was "lately arrived from the Gold Coast,

25. See above, p. 48.

26. *Virginia Gazette* (Purdie and Dixon), April 22, 1773.

27. Ibid., (Purdie and Dixon), September 22, 1768.

28. L. B. Steuart to Benjamin Massiah, July 5, 1751, Steuart Papers, Historical Society of Pennsylvania (Colonial Williamsburg microfilm). This letter comments very interestingly on the preference of merchants and planters for large consignments of slaves.

with a Cargo of choice Slaves." Instead he probably would have joined his neighbors and acquaintances who gathered for a sale held by the sheriff, Frederick Bryan, "at 12 o'clock before the Raleigh Tavern for ready money of Several likely Slaves, to satisfy some executions."[29]

29. *Virginia Gazette* (Purdie and Dixon), March 16, 1767.

CHAPTER VII

A Personal Description of Williamsburg's Negroes

Such details as the physical appearance, dress, or speech of the eighteenth-century slaves may seem almost more subjects of antiquarian curiosity than of real historical consequence. They cannot have mattered greatly to slaveowners who sometimes were hard pressed for an accurate description of one of their Negroes. However, there are a few general points of information that could contribute to the accuracy of any attempt to interpret the life of colonial Williamsburg's slave population.

Physically, the Negroes of the eighteenth century, like the whites of the same period, appear to have been on the average shorter in height than their modern counterparts. Both male and female slaves are sometimes described vaguely as being tall or tall and slim, but the instances are rare in which a Williamsburg slave is specifically estimated to be as tall as six feet.[1] In the largest number of instances adult males were stated to about 5 feet 5 inches or 5 feet 6 inches in height.[2] Examples of slaves either slightly above or below this figure occur about equally so that 5 feet 6 inches is a reasonably accurate estimate of the average height of a full-grown male.

There is little reason to question the fact that the clothing worn by Negroes was ordinarily of the simplest, coarsest variety.[3] One or two other assumptions that are frequently made—that slaves were inadequately clothed for winter weather and that the whites were careless about the outright nakedness of some slaves—have a degree of accuracy but are not uniformly

1. *Virginia Gazette* (Purdie), July 25, 1777.
2. See, for example, Ibid., (Purdie and Dixon), March 24, 1774; (Purdie), March 8, 1776; (Dixon and Hunter), March 23, 1776; July 20, 1776.
3. *The Negro in Virginia.* Compiled by the Writers' Program of the Work Projects Administration (New York, 1940), pp. 71-73.

true. At any one time most slaves probably had little more clothing than what they were actually wearing. At least the occasional advertisements which describe a Negro with extra clothing seem to make a special point of this fact.[4]

In general one feels that the slaves in Williamsburg were reasonably well-clothed. The nature of the work most of them performed required fairly clean and adequate clothing. There are particularly favorable comments on the fact that waiters and cooks in the inns "were dressed neatly and cleanly."[5] To require that "the Negroes at the Better public houses must not wait on you unless in Clean shirts and drawers & feet washed—" more than met, however, the minimum demands of the eighteenth century in matters of cleanliness and dress.[6] Not every traveler was so well satisfied, as Ebenezer Hazard's complaint about the nakedness of Negro children suggests:

The Virginians, even in the City do not pay proper Attention to Decency in the Appearance of their Negroes; I have seen Boys of 10 & 12 Years of Age going through the Streets quite naked, & others with only Part of a Shirt hanging Part of the Way down their Backs. This is so common a sight that even the Ladies do not appear to be shocked at it.[7]

Whenever accounts occur describing the dress of slaves from Williamsburg, the men are typically attired in pants and shirt plus a coat of some type. There is a wide variety of fabrics, though all of coarser types, and a whole rainbow of colors. The pants are once or twice described as short breeches.[8] One of the most interesting variations was a pair worn by a man who had

4. *Virginia Gazette* (Dixon and Nicholson), July 24, 1779.
5. "A Journey from Philadelphia to Charleston, 1783." Virginia State Library, quoted in Raymond B. Pinchbeck, "The Virginia Negro Artisan and Tradesman," *Publications of the University of Virginia*, Phelps-Stokes Fellowship Papers., No. 7 (Richmond, Va., 1926), p. 39.
6. William Hugh Grove Diary, University of Virginia (Colonial Williamsburg photostat.)
7. Fred Shelley, ed., "The Journal of Ebenezer Hazard in Virginia, 1777," *Virginia Magazine of History and Biography*, 62 (October, 1954): 410.
8. *Virginia Gazette* (Dixon and Hunter), March 7, September 5, 1777.

run away so frequently that he was kept in leg irons. His breeches were laced on the side so that they could be worn over the irons.[9] The women seem usually to have worn a petticoat and a dress of simple, colored material, or else they are described as having on a petticoat and a waistcoat.

Much of the lighter clothing for slaves was made from cotton cloth woven in the colony, which was often called "Negro cotton" or "Virginia cloth."[10] A certain amount of "country linen" was also produced here.[11] English osnaburg, a heavy, coarse fabric, was also widely used, as was another heavy material, Russian drab.[12]

In many cases the slaves in Williamsburg, as they did everywhere else, wore old clothes, well-patched and maybe passed down from the master's family.[13] But there were new shirts and jackets interspersed among the worn clothes, and a few slaves appear as very well-dressed.[14] A fifteen-year old boy advertised as a runaway in the winter of 1773 was wearing a new bearskin jacket, blue breeches, country-knit stockings, and a light pair of shoes with straps.[15] Alexander Purdie owned a runaway whom he described as "well-clad in new coat, waistcoat, and breeches, of red duffil, and has a new gray fearnaught great coat."[16]

One of the most misunderstood facts about the Negroes of the eighteenth century is the relative skill with which they spoke English. The logic of the recent importation of so many slaves from Africa plus the impressions that have stemmed from Negro dialects of later years have fostered the idea that very few slaves in the colonial era spoke more than very broken

9. Ibid., May 9, 1745.
10. Ibid., (Purdie), September 6, 1776; October 17, 1777; (Dixon and Hunter), March 21, 1777.
11. Ibid., (Dixon and Hunter), March 21, 1777.
12. Ibid., (Dixon and Hunter), July 20, 1776.
13. Ibid., (Purdie and Dixon), March 31, 1768; (Dixon and Hunter), July 20, 1776; March 21, 1777; September 5, 1777; (Purdie), October 17, 1777.
14. Ibid., (Purdie and Dixon), March 31, 1768; (Dixon and Hunter), March 21, 1777.
15. Ibid., (Purdie and Dixon), January 7, 1773.
16. Ibid., (Purdie), March 8, 1776.

English. This viewpoint also had contemporary support from a few travelers.[17]

Nevertheless, there is a greater weight of evidence for the contrary view that with opportunity and a very little time the Negro learned to speak English clearly.[18] References to Negroes who spoke broken English or did not understand it at all nearly always prove to involve very recent arrivals from Africa.[19] At that, the average imported slave often learned to speak comprehensible English within a few years, like Lewis Burwell's man, Jumper, who had been in the colony two years but could talk "pretty good English."[20]

The level of speech of Negroes born and brought up in the colonies was almost uniformly high.[21] Hugh Jones commented as early as 1724 that "the Native Negroes" were among "the only People [in both England and the colonies] that speak true English."[22] Since so high a proportion of the Williamsburg Negroes were Virginia-born, they should have generally spoken fluent English. A representative example is that of a slave, Peres, who had lived for many years around Williamsburg before eventually becoming the property of George Washington. Peres, one of four slaves who engineered an escape from Washington in 1761, spoke good English, having "little of his Country Dialect left."[23] There were also a number of slaves here who were able to read and write without difficulty.[24] On the whole, this seems to be one more area in which the Negroes in Williamsburg excelled among the slaves of the colony.

17. Cf. J. F. D. Smyth, "Travels in Virginia in 1773," *Virginia Historical Register,* 6 (April, 1853): 82.

18. Allen W. Read, "The Speech of Negroes in Colonial America," *Journal of Negro History,* 24 (July, 1939): 247-58.

19. Ibid.

20. *Virginia Gazette,* April 21, 1738.

21. Read, "Speech of Negroes," pp. 247-58.

22. Grace W. Landrum, "The First Colonial Grammar in English," *William and Mary Quarterly,* 2nd ser., 19 (July, 1939): 282. The work referred to and quoted from is Jones's *Accidence to the English Tongue* (1724).

23. *Maryland Gazette,* August 20, 1761.

24. *Virginia Gazette,* May 9, 1745; (Purdie and Dixon), April 16, 1767; February 21, 1771; (Purdie), December 12, 1777.

CHAPTER VIII

The Social Life of the Negro in Williamsburg

AN OPPRESSED community nearly always has a furtive quality about its life that conceals what its members really think and do and feel among themselves. This is simply a matter of self-preservation, of protecting whatever degree of independence its members still possess. Negro neighborhoods in the South have as often as not retained to the present day vestiges of such a barrier against white intrusions. As slaves the Negroes had even more need of this defense, and there are occasional evidences of the resourcefulness of the slave inhabitants of eighteenth-century Williamsburg in this regard.

No better example exists of the way in which the Negroes who lived here were both an integral part of the busy life of the capital and yet a society that could not be completely comprehended by their masters than the ability of the local Negro community to hide runaways. It is perfectly clear that the Negroes who had lived here any length of time were well known to most of the white residents in the way of all small towns. Advertisers in the *Gazette* often felt it unnecessary to tell more about a Williamsburg slave than the executors of Josiah Royle's estate did about a mulatto girl, Jenny, of whom they stated, "As she is well known in the Neighborhood of this City, a more particular Description is unnecessary...."[1]

Yet Jenny and other Negroes just as well known were runaways who were thought to have remained in hiding in or around Williamsburg. In some cases a master only suspected that his slave had remained here secretly.[2] But there were other instances where slaves had been seen in Williamsburg since

1. *Virginia Gazette* (Dixon and Hunter), January 28, 1775. See also *ibid.*, (Dixon and Nicolson), May 1, 1779.
2. Ibid., (Purdie), March 8, 1776; (Dixon and Hunter), March 23, September 5, 1776.

their "elopement" and still could not be recaptured.[3] Many of these fugitives had relatives or acquaintances in town whom the owners realized were probably hiding the fugitives.[4] William Carter, for instance, stated of his mulatto girl, Venus, who had run away in December of 1766, "I imagine she is either harboured by other slaves in kitchens and quarters in and about town, or else gone for *Nansemond* county, from whence she was purchased a few years ago."[5]

There was also difficulty with slaves who had once lived in Williamsburg and returned as runaways. Edward Cary, Jr. owned an 18-year old female slave raised in York County and leased to Philip Moody in Williamsburg in 1774. The next year Cary hired her out to John Thruston in King and Queen County; but Kate—this was the girl's name—had acquired attachments in Williamsburg that led her to flee Thruston's plantation. As Cary announced, "She has got a husband in *Williamsburg*, and probably may pass for a free person, as she is well acquainted in that city, and I have repeatedly heard of her being there."[6] It hardly seems possible that this slave girl could have been a fugitive almost two years, have been recognized frequently in Williamsburg during that time, and yet not have been recaptured and returned to either Cary or Thruston. Above all, she could hardly have succeeded, unless the slave community had ways and means of shielding its members that the slaveowner could not readily penetrate.

Kate's experiences illustrate another feature of the life of the Negro under slavery. She had run away to Williamsburg in the first place because she had a husband here, an important point for a number of reasons. The customs and practices of eighteenth-century slavery did not usually permit the marriage of slaves, even baptised ones, in any legal or religious sense.[7] Yet for every slave who took advantage of, or was unable to resist, the open invitation to promiscuity inherent in such a situation,

3. Ibid., (Rind), March 7, 1771; (Purdie), September 6, 1776.
4. Ibid., (Purdie and Dixon), September 15, 1768; January 10, 1771.
5. Ibid., (Purdie and Dixon), February 5, 1767.
6. Ibid., (Purdie), November 29, 1776.
7. *The Negro in Virginia.* Compiled by the Writers' Program of the Work Projects Administration (New York, 1940), pp. 79-85.

there were many others who tried under the most difficult conditions to pursue a normal family life. The slaveowners gave a certain recognition to these "marriages," although they often did not hesitate to destroy a slave marriage by selling one mate.

There are even accounts of a sort of marriage ceremony known as "jumping the broomstick," in which the Negro couple stepped across a broomstick together as a symbol of the fact that they considered each other husband and wife. One slave has left a personal recollection of her mother's broomstick marriage. As the mother recounted it to her daughter, the young couple simply decided on a Sunday that they would like to be married. Thereupon they went up to the kitchen and asked to see their master by sending word through the cook. After determining they were old enough—both the boy and the girl were 16 in this instance—the owner readily assented and sent them off to one of the Negro women, Aunt Lucy, who was probably either the midwife or the oldest woman; and she performed the broomstick ceremony. Since it was Sunday and all the Negroes were around their quarters, the old woman called them together immediately. They formed a circle around the couple, while Aunt Lucy recited a few verses from the Bible and laid a broomstick on the floor. The couple locked arms, jumped over the stick, and were then husband and wife in the eyes of the other slaves in the quarter.[8]

The slaveowners understandably preferred to have their Negroes marry on the home plantation to lessen the chance of runaways and to insure that children born to the couple would belong to him. Permission to marry on a neighboring plantation was sometimes granted, though it usually restricted the couple to a single visit a week.[9]

It is only possible to speculate about the problem slave marriages might create in a town such as Williamsburg, where a large number of slaves belonging to many different owners lived in close contact. The number of unions of slaves belonging to different owners undoubtedly increased, and the master's consent was probably much less vital than on an isolated plantation. He was also likely to be able to do far less about

8. Ibid., pp. 81-82.
9. Ibid., p. 84.

destroying a marriage made against his will. These slave marriages may well have been the occasion of a lot of trouble in Williamsburg. Certainly this is the source to which a large number of fugitive slaves can be traced. Edward Cary's Kate, whose flight from King and Queen to Williamsburg has already provided so much by way of illustration, had lived in Williamsburg only a year and yet found a slave to whom she considered herself wed. Gaby, a male slave belonging to James Burwell at King's Creek, was listed twice in three years as a runaway.[10] Both times he had fled into Williamsburg where his wife worked. Slaves brought from some distance and thereby separated from a wife frequently ran off, too—in this case not into hiding around town but back to their original home.[11]

The frustrations that slaveowners experienced in trying to recover slaves in hiding around town seems all the more surprising in the view of the living arrangements for slaves. While our exact knowledge about where slaves lived in Williamsburg is sketchy, we can be reasonably certain they lived on the master's property, perhaps close to the main house where surveillance should have been relatively easy.

The conventional arrangement on the large plantations with one or two rows of crude slave cabins, possibly at some little distance from the plantation house, was more extensive than even the larger town households required. There were Williamsburg properties on which, undoubtedly, an outbuilding or two was used specifically for slave quarters. When a house that had belonged to Peter Randolph was offered for sale, the description pointed out that it included five major outbuildings —two stables, a coach house, a kitchen, and a servant's house of the same dimension as the kitchen.[12] One of the advertisements on runaways refers to "kitchens and quarters in and about town," as if there might have been a fairly large number of slave quarters scattered through Williamsburg.[13] In other

10. *Virginia Gazette* (Purdie and Dixon), September 15, 1768; (Rind), March 7, 1771.

11. Ibid., (Purdie and Dixon), January 8, 1767; (Purdie), October 17, 1777.

12. Ibid., (Purdie and Dixon), October 8, 1767.

13. Ibid., (Purdie and Dixon), February 5, 1767.

cases the living space for slaves seems not to have been a separate building but only the second-floor rooms over the kitchens. Eliza Baker remembered slaves living over the kitchen at the Garrett House in the nineteenth century.[14] Household servants sometimes had no quarters of their own but simply spread pallets in the hall, on the staircase, or somewhere else in the house after the family had retired.[15]

Whatever the arrangement of living quarters for the slaves, they never were provided with much furniture. At best there can hardly have been more than a bed or a cot and maybe a few discarded pieces from the main house.[16] In the specific instance of Williamsburg not a single inventory has appeared that suggests anything definite about the furnishings of slave quarters. The inventory of the William Prentis estate did include a room-by-room listing of furnishings that also included outbuildings. It contains one or two entries of possible value. Described as being "In out House, Yard, &C" were a number of tools, some scrap metal, and a few chairs and chests. These last few pieces of furniture could have been used by the slaves, although no beds at all were included. Also, several items were "*At old Nann[y's?],*" one of Prentis's slaves being called old Nanny. This included only a frying pan, a pot, a grindstone, and a few tools, however, and no furniture at all.[17]

The Negro slave had little time to spend as he wished—usually Saturday nights and Sundays plus additional time at one or two major holidays like Christmas and Whitsunday. Descriptions of plantation life substantially agree about the way in which the slaves spent their spare time. On Saturday nights they usually gathered in the slave quarters for dancing, which was as much their favorite recreation as it was that of most other Virginians.[18] Philip Fithian has described how by five o'clock on Saturday at Nomini Hall "every Face (especially

14. Eliza Baker, "Memoirs of Williamsburg, Virginia," Typescript of conversations between Eliza Baker, an ex-slave, and W. A. R. Goodwin, May 4, 1933, in Colonial Williamsburg Archives, p. 4.
15. *Negro in Virginia*, p. 42.
16. Ibid., pp. 67-69.
17. York County Records, Wills and Inventories, Book 21, p. 253.
18. *Negro in Virginia*, pp. 87-95.

the Negroes) looks festive & cheerful—"[19] Sundays the Negroes might tend their garden plots or spend as much time as possible sleeping and resting.[20]

The slaves in Williamsburg probably enjoyed a social life that cannot have been much different, especially in amount of free time. Despite laws forbidding it, the Negroes here seemed able to procure and consume alcohol in some quantity. The Negro girl described as "fond of Liquor, and apt to sing indecent and Sailors Songs when so" is a good case in point.[21] So is the series of charges and countercharges involving the merchants Daniel Fisher, John Holt, and John Greenhow. Fisher was charged by the other two with selling liquor to Negroes without the written permission of their masters. When the case came into court, Fisher turned on his accusers and claimed that Holt had "without the least scruple whatever" served two Negroes whom Fisher himself had turned away. The aggrieved Fisher also claimed that John Greenhow was "infamously remarkable for trafficking with Negroes in wine, or any other commodity, Sunday not excepted."[22] These accusations involve so much personal bickering and name-calling that acceptance of them at face value is impossible; but their general tenor suggests that a certain amount of dealing with slaves in liquor went on in Williamsburg. Many of the masters may, for one thing, have been lenient at times about issuing permission for their slaves to have intoxicants. William Byrd recounted the well-known instance in which Governor Spotswood could not get his servants to remain sober for a large holiday entertainment at the Palace until they were promised the privilege of getting drunk the next day.[23]

Most of the aspects of life discussed above would have been the private concern of a free person. The slave, of course, had

19. Hunter Dickinson Farish, ed., *Journal and Letters of Philip Vickers Fithian, 1773-1774: A Plantation Tutor of the Old Dominion* (new edn., Williamsburg, Va., 1957), p. 137.

20. Ibid., p. 96.

21. *Virginia Gazette* (Purdie and Dixon), January 20, 1774.

22. "Narrative of George [Daniel] Fisher," *William and Mary Quarterly*, 1st ser., 17 (January, 1909): 148-49.

23. Louis B. Wright and Marion Tinling, eds., *The Secret Diary of William Byrd of Westover, 1709-1712* (Richmond, Va., 1941), p. 298.

no such right. Where he lived, whom he married, and sometimes even what he did for amusement were no more his to
decide than the work he would do or the master he would
serve. Yet by a combination of evasion and defiance the slaves
were often able to achieve some degree of independence in
their social life. Town life, if anything, seemed to increase this
degree of freedom and to create a slave community with its
own thoughts and pleasures and with the means of protecting
its fugitives.

CHAPTER IX

The Humanitarian Impulse:
Religion and Education

1. The Anglican Missionary Effort in Virginia

THE FIRST Negroes brought to Virginia came so largely by accident that there can hardly have been much thought one way or the other about Christianizing them. Religious motives played a part in colonization and in Indian relations, but only in retrospect did they become a justification for the importation of Negroes.[1] Nor were any sizeable number of blacks won to the Christian faith before the end of the colonial era.[2] Yet there were many ways in which religion was to influence the history of the Negro in these years.

At first, when the few Negroes in Virginia were generally regarded as no different from other servants, a number of them were baptized, probably as a matter of course and without much thought on the part of the white settlers that it had any special significance. Anthony and Isabella, two of the Negroes in the original shipment, were married soon after their arrival; and their first child was taken to Jamestown in 1624 and baptized with the name of their master, William Tucker.[3] Another example was Rose, a Negro belonging to Robert Stafford, whose son William was baptized in 1655.[4] In the light of the Spanish Christian names borne by some of the earliest Negroes—the aforementioned Anthony and Isabella, two other

1. Perry Miller, "The Religious Impulse in the Founding of Virginia: Religion and Society in the Early Literature," *William and Mary Quarterly*, 3rd ser., 5 (October, 1948): 492-522; 6 (January, 1949): 24-41.
2. The best general discussion of this is Marcus W. Jernegan, "Slavery and Conversion in the American Colonies," *American Historical Review*, 21 (April, 1916): 504-27.
3. *The Negro in Virginia*. Compiled by the Writers' Program of the Work Projects Administration (New York 1940), p. 10.
4. Joseph B. Earnest, *The Religious Development of the Negro in Virginia* (Charlottesville, Va., 1914), p. 18.

Anthonys, a John Pedro, and others—some of them may have been baptized by the Spanish and then captured and brought to Jamestown.[5] Baptism probably carried some temporal advantages with it, as in the case of John Phillip, a Negro, who in 1624 was permitted to testify as a free man and a Christian because he had been baptized.[6] At the least it made it easier to incorporate the Negroes into the existing system of indentured servitude.[7]

As the status of the Negro began to harden into life servitude, however, the owners became increasingly afraid that baptism might result in freedom for their Negroes.[8] English precedent was not entirely clear, and some planters took the precaution of actively forbidding baptism of Negroes bound for life. In 1667 the Assembly broke the impasse by enacting legislation that baptism did not alter a person's bond or free condition. The same law also encouraged masters to permit capable slaves to be baptized.[9] Subsequently, whether one was black or white began to replace whether was Christian or pagan as the true determinant between free and slave status.[10]

The way now stood clear for the defense of slavery as a Christianizing and civilizing institution. The image of the rude, animal-like African being educated and humanized by the beneficent influences of bondage, not the least of which was religion, became a bulwark of the rationale for slavery.[11] This

5. Helen T. Catterall, ed., *Judicial Cases Concerning American Slavery and the Negro* (Washington, 1924-1926), 1: 54-57.

6. Ibid., p. 76.

7. Ibid., pp. 54-55.

8. Jernegan, "Slavery and Conversion," pp. 504-7.

9. William Waller Hening, ed., *The Statutes at Large Being a Collection of all the Laws of Virginia* (Richmond, Va., etc., 1810-1823), 2:260.

10. Ibid., pp. 283, 490-92; 3: 447-48.

11. Jernegan, "Slavery and Conversion," pp. 504-7. Here, however, the idea is advanced that the justification of slavery as a means of conversion preceded any fear that such conversion would free the Negro and that therefore missionary activity received a temporary setback. But it is doubtful that the argument that slavery offered an opportunity for propagating religious faith really became much of a factor until the status of a slave had been more sharply defined. By that time the possibility that Christianity might convey freedom had been resolved in favor of continued bondage.

argument was not entirely conceived in hypocrisy. Many set out to give substance to the proposition that slavery might be a means of conversion of the Negro, for the English-speaking world was experiencing the dawning of a humanitarian impulse that was to make its full force felt only after 1800.[12] Its roots at this time were religious, and the primary concern of those who worried about the fate of the Negro was that his soul might be saved in the next world by conversion to Christianity in this. To a lesser extent they also wished to educate the slave, though primarily as a means of increasing his capacity for understanding religion.

The intent of the humanitarians in all their endeavors was not even remotely revolutionary. They were in all sincerity striving to improve the existing order. In their aspirations for the Negro they sought only to make slavery more humane, not to eradicate it as fundamentally and irrevocably inhuman. Religious training, they sometimes argued, would actually make the Negro more obedient and more satisfied with his lot.[13]

Almost none of this interest in the slaves originated among colonial slaveowners, and little of it represented governmental policy. The instructions of a new governor normally included a brief exhortation to encourage the conversion of Negroes, but official action just about stopped at that point.[14] The real source of endeavor was the Anglican church. Until late in the eighteenth century the successes in converting and educating the Negro were the results of the church's efforts and the failures were a reflection of the church's limitations for so staggering a task.

The church pursued its interest in the Negro. Through the eighteenth century most of the bishops of London made it a point of special concern; and their commissaries in Virginia, especially James Blair and William Dawson, were in agreement. Sometimes this influence had the desired effect on the

12. George Macaulay Trevelyan, *English Social History* (London, etc., 1947), p. 347.

13. Edgar L. Pennington, "Thomas Bray's Associates' Work Among Negroes" *American Antiquarian Society Proceedings,* new ser., 58 (1938): 334-35.

14. See, for example, *Virginia Magazine of History and Biography,* 21 (October, 1913): 354; 28 (January, 1920): 43.

parish clergy, for more of them than one might have thought were seriously interested in attempting to reach the slaves within their parishes.[15] In the colonies as a whole the Society for the Propagation of the Gospel, from its founding in 1701, expended a part of its missionary effort on the Negro, but very little of its work occurred in Virginia.[16] Dr. Bray's Associates, a smaller group especially interested in schools and libraries, was responsible for the operation of two Negro schools in Virginia.

One of the peak periods of Anglican missionary effort among the Negroes came in the decade of the 1720s, when Edmund Gibson, just consecrated as bishop of London, threw his influence behind the movement. Gibson's correspondence to and from Virginia was filled with discussion of the slaves. One of the key questions in his questionnaire of 1724 to clergymen working in the colonial field was, "Are there any Infidels, bond or free, within your Parish; and what means are used for their conversion?"[17] Three episcopal letters in 1727 on the conversion of Negroes intensified his campaign.[18] There were even proposals to make it economically attractive for the planters to encourage religious instruction for their Negroes by offering to exempt a slave baptized before the age of 14 from the tithe for four years.[19] These years represented probably the most intensive campaign to win the conversion of the slaves at any time prior to the Great Awakening.

Of the clergy who answered Bishop Gibson's set of questions

15. There are summaries of the Anglican effort in Virginia to convert the Negro slaves in Mary F. Goodwin, "Christianizing and Educating the Negro in Colonial Virginia." *Historical Magazine of the Protestant Episcopal Church*, 1 (Sept., 1932):143-52, and in Jerome W. Jones, "The Established Virginia Church and the Conversion of Negroes and Indians, 1620-1760," *Journal of Negro History*, 46 (1961): 12-23. See also Herbert S. Klein, *Slavery in the Americas: A Comparative Study of Virginia and Cuba* (Chicago, 1967), pp. 105-26, which stresses the inability of the Anglican church in Virginia to ameliorate the slaves' lot.

16. Edgar W. Knight, ed., *A Documentary History of Education in the South Before 1860* (Chapel Hill, N.C., 1949-53), 1:63.

17. William Stevens Perry, ed., *Historical Collections Relating to the American Colonial Church* (Hartford, Conn., 1870), 1:261.

18. Jernegan, "Slavery and Conversion," pp. 507-11; Fulham Palace Manuscripts, Virginia, British Transcripts, Library of Congress, II, 109.

19. Perry, *Historical Collections*, 1: 34.

only one or two flatly admitted they were making no effort among the Negroes. The Rev. Owen Jones of St. Mary's in Essex County replied cryptically that in his parish, so far as the conversion of slaves was concerned, "particular means [were] discouraged."[20] The same thing was undoubtedly true of most of the clergy who completely ignored the bishop's query.

The efforts of the more active ministers followed an almost uniform pattern. In the first place, they regarded the newly imported African as beyond their influence, as quite probably he was, unless he had mastered English very quickly. So, for the most part, they confined their efforts to Negroes who had been born in Virginia or had grown up there from early in life.[21] The method of instruction was largely the time-worn one of "preaching and catechising." Quite often there was no special effort to adjust these instructions to the needs and understanding of the Negroes. The slaves were expected to get along on the regular sermons and whatever teaching of the catechism the children of white parishioners received.[22] Usually about the time a slave could recite the catechism and maybe the Apostles' Creed and Lord's Prayer reasonably fluently, he would be baptized.[23] Rarely and in very small numbers, slaves were admitted to the sacrament of the Holy Communion.[24]

Clergymen were careful to avoid the slightest hint of an attack on the institution of slavery. Many of the Virginia clerics were themselves slaveholders, and the church also owned slaves which had been left it as endowments in the wills of deceased Virginians.[25] In their instructions the ministers urged the Negroes to cultivate obedience and patience as virtues becoming a Christian slave. Nothing was left undone to impress upon the slaves that Christianization was not to be confused with freedom in this world. In one instance Negro candidates

20. Ibid., p. 310.
21. Ibid., pp. 264, 280, 283, 287, 293, 297, 312.
22. Ibid., pp. 261, 271, 273, 281, 285, 308.
23. Ibid., pp. 263, 274, 276, 280, 287, 291, 297, 301.
24. Ibid., p. 291.
25. R. W. Marshall, "What Jonathan Boucher Preached," *Virginia Magazine*, 46 (January, 1938): 4-6; Perry, *Historical Collections*, 1: 360-61.

for baptism were required to take a special oath declaring that they did not seek baptism out of any design of freedom.[26]

The church still ran into uncompromising opposition from the slaveowning planters. Occasionally a minister was able to report:

. . . I have prevailed with some of my parishioners to suffer their slaves to be instructed in the christian religion & baptized, for which they have since thank'd me, having found them both more trusty & more diligent in their service than they were before . . .[27]

But he was much more likely, when the subject of baptizing slaves was raised, to find "the owners Generaly not approving thereof, being led away by the notion of their being and becoming worse slaves when Christians."[28] Between the hostility and indifference perhaps a few families remained in a parish who were willing to permit instruction and baptism of slaves.

If the slaveowners needed a justification for their position, they were able to find it in the rumors of a slave insurrection on which Bishop Gibson's first efforts foundered in 1730. The exact details of the incident are difficult to established, as two letters, one from Commissary Blair and one from the governor to the bishop of London, are about the only sources.[29] Both Blair and Gooch denied that there was any well-formed plan of revolt, though Blair conceded that the Negroes had been circulating rumors that baptism would set them free and that they had grown "angry and saucy" when their day of liberation failed to arrive. There had been talk of insurrection and a certain amount of uneasiness on both sides. Then, according to Gooch, trouble appeared to subside for a few weeks only to reappear in Norfolk and Princess Anne counties. There two hundred Negroes gathered to choose leaders for a rising, but an informant revealed their plot with the result that four of the ringleaders were hanged.

26. Pennington, "Thomas Bray's Associates," p. 333.
27. Lawrence De Butts to Bishop of London, July 1, 1722, Fulham Palace Manuscripts, Virginia, I, 133.
28. Perry, *Historical Collections*, 1:315.
29. May 14 and May 28, 1731, Fulham Palace Manuscripts, Virginia, I, 110, 111.

The missionaries were shortly back at work, however, with fresh hopes of converting the slaves. Their plan of attack was still essentially to preach and to catechise, though "in such a plain affecting way as may move their hearers."[30] These clergymen continued to meet strong opposition from their parishioners.[31] But occasionally they had phenomenal successes, as when the Rev. Anthony Gavin, rector of St. James, Goochland, baptized a total of 172 Negroes on a journey through the far reaches of his parish.[32] Examples like this did not occur frequently enough, though, for these men to begin to keep pace with the expanding slave population.

It is easy to conclude that the ultimate failure of the Anglican effort to reach the slaves resulted not only from the hostility of many planters but also from lack of much real spirit among most of the clergy. There is much support for this view in the indifference of someone like the Rev. John Bell, who said of the Negroes in his parish, Christ Church, in Lancaster County, "The Church is open to them, the word preached, and the Sacraments administered with circumspection."[33] Well-intentioned men were sometimes overcome by the immensity of the task the bishop had asked of them and fell into the weariness of Charles Bridges who once wrote to his superior:

The little good I find I am capable of doing without your particular countenance in first subscribing and getting subscription to, that your excellent design of instructing the Negroes here according to the method proposed, and pressing the Commissary to follow you and solicit the Governor and his interest, I say all that can be done in this affair without your charitable efforts, will, to my great concern, I fear come to nothing. The Commissary and I grow in years, and the world hangs heavy upon us. I am rous'd sometimes and then call upon him, and then he is asleep perhaps & answers nothing, & I am ready to sleep too. Would to God your powerful voice

30. Charles Bridges to Bishop of London, October 20, 1735, ibid., II, 40.
31. Adam Dickie to Mr. Newman, June 27, 1732, ibid., III, 39.
32. Perry, *Historical Collections*, 1:360-61.
33. Ibid., p. 283.

would sound in our ears to get up and be doing a little more good, while there is time and opportunity, . . .[34]

There were, of course, ministers of greater zeal and ability laboring in the same cause. Commissary Blair, despite his age, was asleep less than Charles Bridges seemed to think. Adam Dickie in Drysdale Parish, King and Queen County, worked hard, holding separate Sunday morning classes for Negroes, because his white parishioners would not allow their children to recite the catechism in the company of slaves. Moreover his very realistic awareness of the difficulties involved did not diminish his efforts.[35] Almost every parish recorded baptisms in small numbers; and in a few the numbers were surprisingly large, as in Accomac Parish when about two hundred Negroes received baptism within a brief period and in Northampton Parish, where 341 baptisms were once recorded in a single month.[36]

The fact of the matter is that the degree of spirit and sincerity behind the Anglican missionary drive among the slaves is not a matter for easy generalization. One could go on citing contrasting examples of indifference and zeal, but to no real purpose. The character of the church's effort was, in fact, of minor consequence in its failure to win Negroes in large numbers. Had every clergyman in Virginia been tireless in this cause, they still would have ministered to a parish that might well have contained several thousand Negroes. They still would have faced the hostility of many slaveowners, who were little enough concerned about the place of religion in their own lives. They still would have been advocating that the slave live according to a moral code that was almost impossible to follow when and where, for instance, there was no legal marriage.

In the long run, the humanitarians held an illogical position in insisting upon maintaining slavery, even defending it as a moral good, and yet claiming the slave for a religious faith which elevated the worth of a human as high as did Christiani-

34. Ibid., pp. 360-61.
35. Adam Dickie to Mr. Newman, June 27, 1732, Fulham Palace Manuscripts, Virginia, III, 39.
36. Perry, *Historical Collections,* 1:301; Fulham Palace Manuscripts, Virginia, III, 42.

ty. As long as they held this view, they could go on hacking at the edges of the problem, here and there converting a few favored slaves owned by especially humane masters. But there was an ultimate incompatibility between slavery and Christianity. The masters knew it with a sort of hard-headed realism, and the slaves at least sensed it from the frequent spread of rumors about winning freedom through baptism.

2. The Anglican Missionary Effort in Williamsburg

Williamsburg as the capital and residence of the bishop's commissary could never expect to be long out of touch with these currents of Anglican missionary effort. In the years of Bishop Gibson's greatest activity James Blair was serving both as commissary and as rector of Bruton Parish. Replying to the 1724 questionnaire Blair had little to say about any success in converting the slaves, but he assured the bishop of his best efforts in the following terms: "I encourage the baptising & catechising of such of them as understand English, and exhort their Masters to bring them to Church and baptise the infant slaves when the Master or mistress become sureties."[37]

However, Blair and his successors at Bruton seem to have had relatively more success over the years in baptizing a portion of the slave population than did many of the clergy in more rural parishes. Blair's correspondence with the Bishop always took an optimistic note, as when he wrote in 1729:

Your Lo'ps Letter concerning the Instruction of the Negroes has had this good effect, that it has put several Masters and Mistresses upon the Instruction of them. And the Negroes themselves in our Neighbourhood are very desirous to become Christians; and in order to it come and give an Account of the Lords prayer, and the Creed and ten Commandments, and so are baptized and frequent the Church; and the Negro children are now commonly baptized. I doubt not some of the Negroes are sincere Converts; but the far greater part of them little mind the serious part, only are in hopes that they shall meet with so much the more respect, and that some time or other Christianity will help them to their freedom. But I hope their

37. Perry, *Historical Collections*, 1:299.

very coming to church will in time infuse into them some better priciples than they have had.[38]

And again the following year:

There is a very great number of Negroes lately instructed in the Church-catechism; at least in the Lords prayer, the Apostles Creed and the ten Commandments, and baptized, and great numbers of them frequent the Church. Some allege it makes them prouder, and inspires them with thoughts of freedom; but I take this to be rather a common prejudice than anything else.[39]

The parish records of Bruton show specific figures for Negro baptisms during most of the twenty-three years between 1746 and 1768. In all, 980 slaves and a few free Negroes received baptism during 19 of these 23 years.[40] There are two later years during the Revolution when 32 and 69 baptisms respectively took place. Then the number drops to almost nothing. By then the slaves may have been attending the independent Negro church in Williamsburg.[41]

The masters whose names are recorded as having slaves baptized likewise constitute a long and rather representative list. A few had sizeable numbers of their slaves baptized at one time or another. Lewis Burwell with 70 of the Kingsmill slaves baptized from 1747-68 easily led the list. Benjamin Waller had 39 of his slaves baptized between 1746 and 1782; James Shield, 31 between 1747 and 1783; Col. Philip Johnson, 24 between 1747 and 1782; and there were others with almost as many. The college was sponsor for 21 of its slaves. A large number of well-known men also were listed as the owners of smaller numbers of baptized slaves, among them several rectors of the parish; two governors, Gooch and Fauquier; and the treasurer, Robert Carter Nicholas, well-known for his piety.

38. June 28, 1729, Fulham Palace Manuscripts, Virginia, II, 109.
39. July 20, 1730, ibid., I, 131.
40. W. A. R. Goodwin, *Historical Sketch of Bruton Church* (Petersburg, Va., 1903), p. 153.
41. See below, section 5, of this chapter
42. See Goodwin, *Historical Sketch of Bruton Church,* pp. 154-57, for a complete listing of communicants having Negroes baptized in the eighteenth century.

Some of these men were, however, owners of a large number of slaves; and it is doubtful just what percentage of their slaves, or of the whole Negro community of Williamsburg, were afforded religious training and eventual baptism. Here, for example, is a sampling of masters for whom there is both a recorded inventory of their estate and a record of slaves baptized:

	No. of slaves at death	No. of slaves baptized
Alexander Purdie	13	3
Alexander Craig	8	6
Peyton Randolph	28	17
John Prentis	11	0
Matthew Moody	4	4
Thomas Cobbs	4	2
Joseph Valentine	12	2
Mark Cosby	5	2
James Wray	20	12
Frederick Bryan	34	16
Anthony Hay	20	5
Peter Hay	11	2
Nathaniel Crawley	32	12

There are a number of questions which these figures cannot answer, particularly that of how many slaves might have been bought after being baptized; but in only a single instance do the number of baptized slaves actually equal the number belonging to the owner at death. It would seem that slaveowners in Williamsburg, while not as unsympathetic to the baptism of their slaves as some of the planters, still encouraged the step for only a portion of their Negroes. A thousand Negro baptisms in twenty years is large enough, however, to prove that the clergy of Bruton Parish did put forth some effort and that the slaveowners of the parish were not always openly hostile to religious instruction of slaves.

3. The Associates of Dr. Bray

Education in eighteenth-century Virginia was at best a haphazard process, even for the children of white parents who were financially able to provide for the instruction of their children. It followed that formal education for Negroes was all but nonexistent. It was possible for the boys of free Negro parents to be bound as apprentices on about the same basis as white children. The surviving indentures for free Negroes are largely identical with those of white apprentices in their requirements of adequate training in the master's craft and instructions in reading and writing.[43] Then, too, the same group of humanitarians who labored for the religious conversion of the Negro sought to give him at least enough education to comprehend simple religious training.

There is, for example, some evidence of interest in education for Negroes in Williamsburg as early as the 1740s. It is Commissary Dawson's name alone, however, which figures in the available evidence. On Dec. 22, 1743 he wrote to England asking for a copy of school rules "which, with some little Alteration, will suit a Negro School in our Metropolis, when we shall have the Pleasure of seeing One established. . . ."[44] Then only a few years later, in 1750, he wrote the bishop of London about Negro schools, "There are three such schools in my parish, these I sometimes visit."[45] Whether these were no more than occasional catechism classes or more regular instruction is a complete mystery, though it hardly seems likely that they could have had a very long history without attracting wider notice. Perhaps one of them was taught by an Elizabeth Wyatt who billed Dawson's estate £1.6 in October, 1754, for schooling his Negro girl, "Jinny," one year.[46]

In the 1760s the English philanthropic group known as Dr.

43. *William and Mary Quarterly*, 1st ser., 8 (October, 1899): 82; *Virginia Magazine*, 2 (April, 1895): 429.
44. To William Newman, December 22, 1743, Dawson Papers, 1728-1775, Manuscripts Division, Library of Congress. (Colonial Williamsburg microfilm.)
45. W. A. R. Goodwin, *The Record of Bruton Parish Church* (Richmond, Va., 1941), p. 34.
46. Dawson Papers, Library of Congress.

Bray's Associates decided Williamsburg was worth a try as the location of one of its schools for Negro children. Out of this effort came a school about which we know something more than we do about earlier ones. Before his death in 1730 Thomas Bray, who had already been a leader in establishment of the Society for the Propagation of the Gospel, named a group of trustees to work with him "amongst the Poorer sort of people, as also among the Blacks and Native Indians." After their founder's death the group decided to perpetuate itself as the Associates of Dr. Bray. In time it came to concentrate its efforts on supplying libraries for Anglican parishes in America and in providing education for Negro children.[47]

The Associates at one time or another founded, or attempted to found, Negro schools in a number of towns and cities throughout the American colonies. The most successful one operated in Philadelphia, for it was strong enough to reopen after the Revolution and continue into the nineteenth century.[48] None of the others came near this record, but the school in Williamsburg operated as long and as successfully as any of the remaining ones.

It was at a meeting of the Associates on January 17, 1760, in the usual London gathering place, "At the Angle Ave Mary Lane," that the project for the school in Williamsburg, together with ones in New York and Newport, was first proposed.[49] The suggestion as to locations came from Benjamin Franklin, who two weeks earlier had taken his place as a newly elected member of the Associates.[50] Also on Franklin's recommendation, William Hunter, postmaster in Williamsburg and printer of the *Virginia Gazette*, and Thomas Dawson, president of William

47. Pennington, "Thomas Bray's Associates," pp. 315-26. See also H. P. Thompson, *Thomas Bray* (London, 1954), especially pp. 98-99.

48. Pennington, "Thomas Bray's Associates," pp. 369-81.

49. Knight, *Documentary History of Education*, 1: 141. For convenience of reference, this and many subsequent citations to the records of Dr. Bray's Associates are from the printed text, edited by Edgar W. Knight. Colonial Williamsburg, however, also possesses microfilm copies of the original records from the archives of the Society for the Propagation of the Gospel in Foreign Parts.

50. Ibid.

and Mary and rector of Bruton Parish Church, were asked to become trustees for the Williamsburg school.

At the same meeting the Associates instructed one of their members, the Rev. James Waring, to prepare a shipment of books for each of the schools.[51] The books which were apparently sent in this first shipment included the following:

50 Child's First Book
40 English Instructor
25 Catechism broke into Short Questions
10 Easy Method of instructing Youth
 2 Preliminary Essays on the Exposition of the Catechism
 3 Indian instructed
 5 Bacons 4 Sermons addressed to the Planters
 2 Bacons 2 Sermons addressed to the Negroes
10 Christians Guide
12 Friendly Admonistions to the Drinkers of Spirit. Liq.
 3 Church Catechism with tracts of Scripture
    Allens Discourses
    Brays Lectures
    Kettelwell's Practical Believer (bound together)
20 Sermons before the Trustees & Associates (by Bruce, Thoresby, King, Ridley)[52]

It fell to the local trustees for the proposed schools to do far more than lend their prestige to the undertaking or perhaps make an occasional inspection. In Williamsburg, for example, Hunter and Dawson had to organize the school, find a teacher and place for it to meet, and supervise its day-to-day operation. Since Thomas Dawson died just as the school in Williamsburg opened, Hunter undertook most of the responsibilities connected with the establishment of the school.

He engaged as a teacher Mrs. Anne Wager, who was to be

51. Ibid., p. 142.
52. Minutes of Dr. Bray's Associates, Catalogue of Books for Home and Foreign Libraries, Manuscripts of Dr. Bray's Associates, S.P.G. Archives.

the only instructor the school ever had.[53] The Associates had decided that £20 sterling would be an adequate salary, but Hunter thought she should have £30 out of which she would have to pay the rent on a suitable house for herself and the school.[54] Dawson had wished to raise the extra £10 by a subscription in Williamsburg, but after his death Hunter asked that it be furnished out of the funds of the Associates.[55] Hunter also decided to accept only 24 scholars rather than the 30 which had been recommended. On Michaelmas, 1760, the Williamsburg school was able to begin operation.[56]

At their November 6, 1760 meeting the Associates approved the change in salary which Hunter had recommended for Mrs. Wager and followed another suggestion of his by asking Robert Carter Nicholas to become a trustee of the Williamsburg school in the place of Dawson. Then Hunter soon died, too; and the Rev. William Yates became a trustee.[57] At the death of Yates in 1764 the Rev. James Horrocks succeeded him as trustee, followed subsequently by Josiah Johnson and John Bracken.[58] It was the treasurer of the colony, Nicholas, however, who served longest and who became the most active trustee. His reports reached the Associates in London with considerable regularity; and, all in all, whatever success the Williamsburg school recorded owed much to his efforts.

Nicholas's first letter to the Associates was written on September 17, 1762. He had been to talk to Mrs. Wager, had looked into the condition of the school, and had decided matters stood about as they did at the time of Hunter's last report. But there is a tone of guarded pessimism in Nicholas's opinions, and he warned the Association that he had no

---

53. We know little about Mrs. Wager. She was elderly, possibly the widow of Thomas Wager who died in Williamsburg in 1725. Her son-in-law was Matt Hatton, a carpenter who owned four lots on Capitol Landing Road and who received the wages still due her after her death. Mary A. Stephenson, "Notes on the Negro School in Williamsburg," Manuscript Report, Colonial Williamsburg Research Dept., pp. 5-6.

54. Knight, *Documentary History of Education*, 1:165-66.

55. Ibid., p. 162.

56. Ibid., pp. 165-66.

57. Ibid., pp. 143-44.

58. Stephenson, "Notes on Negro School," p. 3.

"sanguine expectations" of the school's success.[59] However, the school apparently did very well over the next few years, and it was not long before Nicholas and Yates were writing that the students had 'rather exceeded their Expectations.'"[60]

The minutes and correspondence of the Associates contain a clear picture of a number of phases of the operation of the school. It met, as William Hunter originally planned, in a house rented for both the school and living quarters for the teacher. The trustees, however, took over responsibility for renting the building rather than giving Mrs. Wager an extra allowance for that purpose. From 1763 to 1765 they engaged a house owned by Dudley Digges and possibly located on the northeast corner of Henry and Ireland Streets, for which they paid £8 a year. It proved too small, and in the latter part of 1765 the school moved to a house of John Blair, for which the trustees agreed to pay £12 yearly. Here it remained until its discontinuance.[61]

The best indication we have of the course of study and the methods of teaching employed in the school comes from the rules that Nicholas and Yates drew up in 1762 for the guidance of the schoolmistress.[62] She was to take only scholars approved by the trustees, open the school at seven o'clock in the winter and at six in the summer, enforce regular attendance, and keep her pupils "diligently to their Business during the Hours of Schooling." There were a number of rules governing religious instruction and worship: the teacher should see that her charges learned to read the Bible, she could catechize them according to the doctrines of the Church of England, she should take them to church regularly, and she should conduct prayers in the school. The teacher was also expected to insist upon personal cleanliness, neatness of dress, and moral behavior from the students. Finally, she was to "teach her Scholars the true Spelling of Names, make them mind their Stops & en-

59. Knight, *Documentary History of Education*, 1:165-66.
60. Ibid., pp. 152-53.
61. Stephenson, "Notes on Negro School," p. 4, App. I, citing Manuscripts of Dr. Bray's Associates, American Papers, 1735-1774, S.P.G. Archives, London.
62. Robert Carter Nicholas and William Yates to [John Waring], September 30, 1762, Manuscripts of Dr. Bray's Associates, American Papers, 1735-1774.

deavour to bring them to pronounce & read distinctly." While the school thus laid a heavy emphasis on religion and to that extent resembled the simple classes sometimes conducted by the parish clergy, it is still clear from the emphasis on reading and writing and also from Nicholas's desire to require attendance for a minimum of three years that the intention was to provide a reasonable amount of formal academic training. The scholars, moreover, learned quite readily when left at school long enough, for Nicholas found that the ones who did remain for an adequate time were able "to read pretty well."[63] The trustees likewise appeared satisfied with Mrs. Wager's capabilities as a teacher.[64]

There seemed to be no difficulty in finding pupils for the school. At the request of the Associates, Nicholas raised the enrollment of the school from 24 back to 30, and it remained close to, or a little above, that figure for the duration of the school.[65] The backers of the school never reported the same hostility to the idea of educating young slaves among residents of Williamsburg that they found among some planters who frankly expressed their fear of increasing the understanding of slaves.[66] Lists of the students and their masters survive for the years 1762, 1765, and 1769, the first of these also indicating the ages of the pupils. Most were 6 to 8 years of age, a few as young as 3, and one or two as old as 9 and 10. The masters who enrolled slaves in the school—some thirty or more in these years—represent a good cross section of political leaders like John Blair, Robert Carter Nicholas, and John Randolph and of craftsmen, shopkeepers, and innkeepers like Anthony Hay, Hugh Orr, Alexander Craig, and Jane Vobe. The college also enrolled two of its slaves in 1769, and three of the children in 1762 and two in 1769 were free.[67]

Finances were never a major obstacle while the Negro school was in operation except for the occasional complaints of both Hunter and Nicholas at the high cost of renting a school

---

63. Knight, *Documentary History of Education,* 1:159.
64. Ibid., pp. 150, 156.
65. Ibid., pp. 150, 158, 159.
66. Ibid., pp. 152-53.
67. Stephenson, "Notes on Negro School," App. I, pp. iii-iv.

building. The Associates continued to supply annual payment of £30 toward the expenses of the school, which was £10 more than they had originally planned, until their meeting of March 3, 1768, when they voted to reduce their grants to £25.[68] Robert Carter Nicholas promised in his letter of January 1, 1770, that the people of Williamsburg would meet any additional expense.[69] The treasurer mentioned in 1772 that "some few of the Inhabitants do join with him in contributing towards support of the school, tho' there is far from a general disposition to promote its success."[70] Additional expenses beyond the amount of the grant from the Associates would appear to have been very small. In the years when the trustees were paying £8 rent, they paid Mrs. Wager £28 yearly, making a total expenditure of £36, or £6 over the allotment received from England. After the rental of the larger house at £12, the teacher's salary apparently dropped to £20, making a slightly reduced expenditure of £32 yearly.[71]

The turnover in students remained the most persistent problem the school faced. The slaveowners in Williamsburg had been willing enough to send their slave children to classes, but in too many cases it turned out to be more for the benefit of a cheap nursery than out of more generous motives. As Nicholas reported: "The Owners, as soon as the Children are able to do little offices about the House, either take them away from School entirely, or keep them from it at Times so that they attend only when there is no employment for Them at Home."[72] Hence, he found few scholars remaining for the three years that he considered an absolute minimum.

A rather vague and mysterious problem arose in connection with enforcing the rules adopted for the school by the Associates. Robert Carter Nicholas spoke of these rules as a "very difficult Business" and mentioned the great need of delicacy in handling the situation, "however strange it may appear."[73]

68. Knight, *Documentary History of Education*, 1:162.
69. Ibid.
70. Ibid., p. 164.
71. Stephenson, "Notes on Negro School," App. I, pp. i-ii.
72. Knight, *Documentary History of Education*, 1:159.
73. Ibid., p. 156.

There was a more comprehensible problem in the increasing age and infirmity of the teacher, Mrs. Wager. Nicholas always hoped to find a successor for her; but apparently he never could locate anyone as satisfactory. By December 1771 the mistress's health was bad enough that she had lost considerable time from school.[74] Finally it was Mrs. Wager's death in 1774 that caused the Williamsburg school to be closed.[75]

It has been charged that the expositions of the catechism, testaments, psalters, sermons, and various guides for youth included were "entirely unfitted for the people whom it was intended to benefit."[76] However, the list also included instruction books designed for Indians, beginning English texts, and other works which were probably the best available texts for the kind of elementary instruction planned. It is difficult to see what the Associates would have chosen, if not these.[77]

From time to time the Bray Associates tried to support schools among the Negro population elsewhere in Virginia. There was considerable correspondence back and forth with two ministers in particular, the Rev. James Marye of Orange County and the Rev. Jonathan Boucher of Hanover and later Caroline County.[78] Both these men received shipments of books for use among the large slave populations of their parishes. Neither felt their parishes were compact enough to support an organized school, though Boucher occasionally employed educated Negroes to teach, under his supervision, a few slaves in their own neighborhood from books supplied by him.

Following the successful opening of the Williamsburg school, the Associates hoped they might establish two others at Norfolk and Yorktown.[79] However, no one was willing to do the work that William Hunter and Robert Carter Nicholas had performed in the capital, and no school opened at either place. In

74. Ibid., pp. 163, 164.

75. Pennington, "Thomas Bray's Associates," pp. 360-61.

76. Goodwin, "Christianizing and Educating the Negro," p. 152.

77. Minutes of Dr. Bray's Associates, Catalogue of Books for Home and Foreign Libraries, Manuscripts of Dr. Bray's Associates, S.P.G. Archives.

78. Knight, *Documentary History of Education*, 1: 144-49, 150, 154-57, 160-61.

79. Ibid., p. 149.

Fredericksburg, in which the Associates became interested on the advice of Marye, Fielding Lewis undertook the establishment of a school. Modeled closely on the one in Williamsburg and using the rules Robert Carter Nicholas had prepared, it opened in 1765 with 16 children. The scholars were all quite young, but Lewis was able to write that they "begin already to read prettily."[80]

The Fredericksburg school ran into precisely the same difficulty as the one at Williamsburg. The owners would not leave their young slaves enrolled long enough for adequate training. Lewis actually wanted to keep them five years, but he would have been happy to settle for two or three years.[81] Moreover, he ran into difficulty never encountered at Williamsburg of keeping the enrollment at a desired minimum. There were 17 scholars in 1766 but only 9 in the fall of 1768; and during the preceding summer regular attendance had dropped to 4. The few who did attend were learning to read well but were leaving school as soon as they had mastered this accomplishment.[82] After five years of operation Lewis closed the school because of the small attendance.[83]

When all of the educational activities in Virginia of the Associates of Dr. Bray are added together, the sum comprises an honest and respectable effort. Yet it takes only a minute's reflection to realize how little their work affected the vast Negro population of eighteenth-century Virginia. A few young Negroes in Williamsburg, an even smaller number in Fredericksburg plus a few of the Negroes in maybe three or four rural parishes—these are not much more than the exceptions which prove the rule that educational opportunities for the Negro slaves were all but nonexistent.

Yet, above all the other efforts, the Negro school at Williamsburg stands out as a rather notable thing. Although the entire life of the school was not quite fifteen years, it was at the very least a moderate success. Classes operated at capacity even in the face of too brief an attendance from most of the scholars.

80. Ibid., pp. 158-59.
81. Ibid., p. 160.
82. Ibid., p. 162.
83. Ibid., p. 163.

If not always for the best motives, the masters displayed a willingness to have some of their young slaves educated at the school. What may be most significant of all is the indisputable fact that some of the scholars were learning to read and write, even under relatively adverse conditions. If nothing else, these young scholars had proved the slave's capacity for education.

4. The Negro and The Great Awakening

Beginning about the middle of the eighteenth century with the development of Presbyterianism and continuing on through the appearance of Methodists and Baptists, the religious revival known as the Great Awakening began to sweep through Virginia.[84] To some extent it was strongest in the western areas, where the Negro population was smallest; but these Protestant groups also developed a following in the piedmont and coastal areas. It was not long before their evangelistic efforts embraced the Negroes; and ultimately, in the years following the Revolution, the churches that grew out of the Great Awakening won the loyalty of the overwhelming number of Christianized slaves.

The conventional view has been that the missionary effort among the Negro slaves which was produced by the Great Awakening completely displaced the feebler Anglican efforts.[85] One Negro historian regarded the Great Awakening as the first real impulse for the conversion of the Negro.[86] Certainly there were many points which favored the new religious groups. Their clergy possessed a fervor and a drive that all too many ministers of the established church had lost. The form of worship in their churches included an emotional appeal that was more effective with many slaves. The requirements for baptism, turning more on an aroused religious feeling than an understanding of even the simplest catechism, were much easier for the average slave to satisfy. What also may have

84. The standard work is Wesley M. Gewehr, *The Great Awakening in Virginia* (Durham, N.C., 1930).

85. Gewehr, *Great Awakening in Virginia*, p. 235, although note that on the basis of one letter Gewehr makes the unwarranted implication that the Anglicans generally opposed baptizing slaves.

86. Luther P. Jackson, "Religious Development of the Negro in Virginia from 1760 to 1860," *Journal of Negro History.* 16 (April, 1931): 170-75.

counted for much was the attitude of those slaveowners who were themselves converted in the Great Awakening. Far from opposing the baptism of their slaves, they usually were inclined to encourage it.[87] The Anglican parishes were also too disorganized by the time of the Revolution to remain a real competitor.

Yet, in the period before the Revolution, it is questionable whether the churches of the Great Awakening evidenced much more interest or achieved any greater success than had the Anglicans. The basic similarity, in fact, in the approach to work among the slaves by the Presbyterians, the first of the churches of the Great Awakening to become active in Virginia, and by the Anglicans is far more striking than their differences.

Samuel Davies was one of the more successful Presbyterian ministers in his appeals to slaves. In 1750 he wrote that he had baptized 40 Negroes in a year and had a hundred among his congregation.[88] A few years later he had a regular Negro following of perhaps 300, of which about a third were baptized.[89] Yet large-scale baptism of slaves was not unknown among Anglicans. Jonathan Boucher had baptized 108 Negro children and 30 or 40 adults from the time of his arrival through 1762.[90] Then on the Whitmonday holiday of 1767 he baptized 315.[91] Davies and one or two other Presbyterian leaders were also active in the operation of a school for Negroes, largely supported by backers in London, that immediately suggests a parallel with the schools of the Bray Associates.[92] Davies's personal views on slavery thoroughly accorded with those of the vast majority of Anglican clergymen. Slavery,

87. See, for example, "Journal of Col. James Gordon of Lancaster County, Va.," *William and Mary Quarterly*, 1st ser., 11 (1902-1903): 108-12, 222-23.

88. Perry, *Historical Collections*, 1:369.

89. Gewehr, *Great Awakening in Virginia*, pp. 235-36. See also George William Pilcher, *Samuel Davies, Apostle of Dissent in Colonial Virginia* (Knoxville, Tenn., 1971), pp. 107-16.

90. Knight, *Documentary History of Education*, 1:154-55.

91. Ibid., pp. 160-61.

92. Earnest, *Religious Development of the Negro in Virginia*, pp. 41-42.

he held, did not destroy spiritual freedom; and conversion therefore did not require the emancipation of slaves.[93]

This very real similarity between the position of Samuel Davies and that of representative opinion among Anglican clergymen should not obscure the fact that the established church regarded the work of the Presbyterian leader with abhorrence.[94] Davies had published a small book, *The Duty of Christians*, dealing in very moderate terms with the obligation of masters to instruct their slaves in religion; and this publication became a particular object of attack.[95]

However, there were influences at work in the dissenting churches that led many of their followers to a more questioning attitude on slavery. Much of this development occurred after ideas about slavery had been colored by the natural rights philosophy of the Revolution. At that, none of the Great Awakening churches ever took a consistent stand against slavery. Of all the religious groups in Virginia before 1800 only the Quakers went that far. However, through the 1780s both the Baptists and Methodists were involved in controversies over slavery. The closest either came to an official condemnation of slaveholders was the declaration of 1784 requiring all Methodists in the United States to free their slaves. This remained in force only one year and was not even then effectively enforced.[96] But both churches contained sizeable groups of ministers and laymen who manumitted their own slaves. Large slaveowners such as the Baptists David Barrow and Robert Carter were involved, as well as lesser owners like the group of Methodists of Sussex County who freed nearly 100 slaves at a single court session during the revival of 1787-1788.[97]

After the Revolution the Methodists and Baptists, and to a lesser extent the Presbyterians, far outstripped the remnant of Episcopalians in work among the Negroes. By 1790, when about one Negro in 23 in Virginia was a church member, over

93. Gewehr, *Great Awakening in Virginia*, pp. 236-37.
94. Ibid., pp. 85, 96.
95. *William and Mary Quarterly*, 2nd ser., 1 (Oct., 1921): 280-81.
96. Gewehr, *Great Awakening in Virginia*, pp. 245-46.
97. Ibid., p. 249. See also *Virginia Magazine*, 4 (Jan., 1897): 281.

eighty percent of them were Baptists and Methodists.[98] Initially most of them became members of predominantly white congregations under white leadership. Except for a few isolated cases, they sat in special sections of the church and had no real voice in congregational affairs. In short, for all the supposed democratizing influences of the Great Awakening, there was no difference in the status of these Negroes and those who had attended Anglican churches before the Revolution, except that somewhat more of them were baptized church members.

5. The Negro Baptist Church in Williamsburg

One development was taking place in the churches of the Great Awakening that was eventually to be of great consequence in the religious history of the Negro. By the 1780s a number of Negro preachers had appeared who were beginning to develop a devoted following among their people. Among these were two itinerants, Lewis and Harry Hosier, and also two men, one called Moses and the other Gowan Pamphlet, through whom the Great Awakening made its impact on the Negro community of Williamsburg.[99]

The efforts of these two men, especially Pamphlet, resulted in the establishment of a Negro Baptist Church in Williamsburg that was one of the earliest all-Negro congregations in the United States. The claim has sometimes been made that it was the first Negro church in the country, but like so many "firsts" it is not an easy matter to substantiate.[100] So much of the information about this particular church is a well-blended mixture of tradition and fact that it is difficult to winnow out the true account of its establishment.[101]

Logically the church must have had its beginning in informal meetings at which Moses and Gowan Pamphlet preached. The meetings may well have been secret, as Moses was frequently

98. Jackson, "Religious Development of the Negro in Virginia from 1760 to 1860," pp. 179-80.

99. Ibid., pp. 175-76.

100. See Earnest, *Religious Development of the Negro in Virginia*, p. 54, for an assertion that the Williamsburg congregation was the first Negro church.

101. Probably the most reliable account is that in Robert B. Semple, *A History of the Rise and Progress of Baptists in Virginia*, a work almost

arrested and whipped for holding them.[102] There is a tradition that the meetings began at Green Spring, then shifted to a spot known as Raccoon Chase, and then about 1776 began to take place in Williamsburg.[103]

By the time that Pamphlet had come from Middlesex County and begun to preach to the Williamsburg group, the Baptist leaders in the state had forbidden Negroes to do so. However, Pamphlet defied the church leadership by continuing to preach and to baptize with the result that, for a time, he was under a sentence of excommunication.

With the backing of his baptized followers, who seemed to number about 330, Pamphlet formed an organized church and became its pastor.[104] Even though it came at a time when the congregation and its pastor were out of favor with the white Baptists, this foundation under Pamphlet's leadership would appear to be the real beginning of the Williamsburg group as an organized church. There is some variation in impressions about the date of formation of Pamphlet's congregation. The present-day church claims the date 1776.[105] It has also been put at 1781 on the strength of a citation to Asplund's *Register* for 1794; the date 1785 has also been given.[106] What seems most likely is that the informal meetings of Negroes may have begun around 1776 but that any formal organization of the congregation did not take place before the 1780s.

Despite its insurgent status the church prospered over the next few years. Membership climbed to around 500; and since the congregation included a number of literate members, writ-

---

contemporary with the early Negro church here and one which went through many nineteenth-century editions. The one of 1894, revised and extended by G. W. Beale (Richmond, Va., 1894), has been used in this study.

102. Ibid., p. 148.

103. See folder issued by First Baptist Church, Williamsburg, Va., copy in Colonial Williamsburg Archives.

104. Semple, *History of Baptists*, pp. 118-19, 148.

105. Folder issued by First Baptist Church, Williamsburg, Va., copy in Colonial Williamsburg Archives.

106. Jackson, "Religious Development of the Negro in Virginia from 1760 to 1860," p. 189; Earnest, *Religious Development of the Negro in Virginia*, p. 54.

ten church records were kept.[107] Then, in 1791, peace was restored with the Virginia Baptists, when the congregation petitioned for admittance into the Dover Association.[108] A meeting of the association in Mathews County, which received the petition of Pamphlet's flock, appointed a group of visitors; and at the meeting of October 12, 1793, the Dover Association accepted the Williamsburg church into full membership.[109]

Within the next few years Gowan Pamphlet died, and the church was without a regular pastor.[110] The subsequent history of this congregation in the first two or three decades of the nineteenth century becomes difficult to establish. Sometime in those years Pamphlet's original church went out of existence, to be revived later as the First Baptist Church.[111] So, while the present-day Negro church claims direct descent from Pamphlet's group, there was a break in continuity. Likewise, the Negro church began in the nineteenth century, perhaps very early in it, to use the property on Nassau Street between Duke of Gloucester and Francis Streets, where the present-day First Baptist Church occupied an 1855 structure until its recent demolition.

What happened to Pamphlet's church and its successor in the nineteenth century need not concern us so much, however, as the circumstances under which this congregation was originally established. It was probably the first manifestation of the spirit of the Great Awakening in Williamsburg, and there seems no reason to deny it a place as at least one of the earliest Negro churches in the country. But Gowan Pamphlet's group has an additional significance that goes beyond the mere date of establishment; for, unlike many of the other early Negro churches, it was from the beginning an all-Negro congregation founded without white assistance and, in fact, in defiance of white control.[112]

107. Semple, *History of Baptists*, p. 148.
108. Ibid.
109. Ibid., p. 126.
110. Ibid., pp. 118-19.
111. Ibid., p. 148n.
112. The Petersburg and Norfolk churches, two of the other early Virginia Negro churches, developed out of congregations that were originally mixed. Jackson, "Religious Development of the Negro in Virginia from 1760 to 1860," pp. 189-90.

CHAPTER X

The Law and the Negro

1. Colonial Black Codes

THE EVOLUTION of the Negro's legal status from ordinary indentured servant to servant for life to slave was followed by the development of a separate legal code, distinct trial procedures, and harsher punishments for Negroes accused of criminal acts. Inevitably the slave's lack of personal freedom would have necessitated some revision in the English legal system that had been transported to Virginia. But it was unrelenting fear of the Negro as a potential insurrectionist and constant determination to police his conduct rigidly that instigated most of the early laws affecting Negro slaves.

Only in the last two decades of the seventeenth century did anything more than the faintest beginning of a separate criminal law for Negroes begin to appear. An act of 1680 for preventing Negro insurrections was the first real "'black code" in Virginia, providing specific punishments for the three crimes of leaving the master's property without permission; lifting a hand against a "Christian," that is, a white man; and for hiding or resisting capture after running away.[1] Conviction on the last charge required the death penalty. A 1691 statue that was of the greatest importance as the first legal restriction on manumission of slaves in Virginia also provided a systematic plan for raising a force of men to recapture "outlying slaves," or runaways who were in hiding.[2] Then in 1692 the legislature provided the first trial procedures, in particular the denial of jury trial, which applied specifically to Negro slaves.[3]

There were three more-or-less comprehensive pieces of legislation in the eighteenth century covering the trial, punishment, and regulation of slaves. The first passed in 1705 to be

1. William Waller Hening, (ed.), *The Statutes at Large Being a Collection of all the Laws of Virginia* (Richmond, Va., etc., 1810-1823), 2: 481-82.
2. Ibid., 3: 86-88.
3. Ibid., pp. 102-3.

replaced in 1723 by one which was in turn superseded by the act of 1748.[4] These were the basic codes for the later colonial period, and most of the other legislation affecting Negro crimes, with the exception of laws dealing with runaways, was not much more than a minor modification of the latter two measures.

As has already been suggested, the first law aimed at a crime by Negroes other than running away was the 1680 statute designed to prevent insurrections by punishing slaves who left their master's property without permission or resisted a white man in any way.[5] On the supposition that this act went unnoticed the Assembly required two years later that it be read twice a year in every church.[6] The more comprehensive statute of 1723 sought new safeguards against an armed rising by withdrawing the privilege of benefit of clergy from Negroes convicted of plotting or attempting such rebellion and by forbidding all assemblies of slaves that were not licensed by the masters and held for public worship.[7] It also denied all Negroes free or slave the right to possess weapons, except that free Negroes who were householders or militiamen might keep a single gun and Negroes residing on the frontier might be licensed by the justice of the peace to carry arms.[8] All of these restrictions continued in force under the law of 1748.[9]

Most crimes other than running away or rising in rebellion that a Negro might commit were actions defined in laws that applied equally to all persons in the colony. It is revealing, however, that two felonies, hog stealing and the administration of poisonous medicines, were the occasion of special provisions dealing exclusively with slaves. Hog stealing reached the point that on the third conviction it became a capital offense without benefit of clergy.[10] Such were the risks involved in the temptations of the delicate flavor of roast pig.

The restriction of poisonous medicines obviously arose out of

4. Ibid., 3: 447-62; 4: 126-34; 6: 104-12.
5. Ibid., 2: 481-82.
6. Ibid., pp. 492-93.
7. Ibid., 4: 126-34.
8. Ibid.
9. Ibid., 6: 104-12.
10. Ibid., pp. 122-23.

the belief of the whites that a great many Negroes continued to practice the witchcraft and tribal medicine they had brought from Africa both in honest, if primitive, attempts to cure ailing slaves but also in malicious attempts to destroy an enemy. One section of the 1748 code provided capital punishment for Negroes who prepared and administered medicine of any sort, unless their owner had consented.[11] Benefit of clergy was allowable only where the slave could prove there had been no evil intent. In the wave of Negro crimes which David Mays described in Caroline County from 1761-1764 there were no less than three trials under this law in a three months period during 1762 with convictions in two of them.[12]

Beginning with the legislation of 1692 a separate court procedure developed for the trial of Negroes differing markedly in its rapid movement to trial and lack of constitutional guarantees from that accorded the free man. In capital cases the core of this process was (1) the immediate imprisonment of the slave, (2) issuance by the governor of a commission of oyer and terminer to persons in the county involved to arraign and indict the offender and to take for evidence the confession of the accused or the oaths of two witnesses, or one in some cases, and (3) "without the sollemnitie of jury" to pass such judgment as the law allowed.[13] Throughout the colonial era there was but one modification in this method of trial. In 1765 the governor was permitted to issue general commissions of oyer and terminer to four or more justices of the peace in each county, including one of the quorum, thereby eliminating the necessity of a special commission for each trial.[14]

Initially the procedure for trying slaves did not provide for testimony by other Negroes. In 1723, however, it became permissible in capital cases involving Negroes to take such testimony from Negroes, Indians, or mulattoes "as shall seem convincing," wording which clearly implied that they were not to be accepted as sworn witnesses nor to be questioned at all,

11. Ibid., p. 105.
12. David J. Mays, *Edmund Pendleton, 1721-1803; A Biography* (Cambridge, Mass., 1952), 1: 42-44.
13. Hening, *Statutes*, 3: 102-3.
14. Ibid., 8: 136-37.

except when absolutely necessary.[15] However, this provision for the use of slave testimony in 1723 may have been an opening wedge for employing Negro witnesses far more widely than the law intended. For a new law of 1732 stated that no Negro, mulatto, or Indian should be admitted in court, be sworn as a witness, or give evidence in a case—practices which the law complained had been allowed, even in the General Court—except in the trial of a slave for a capital offense.[16] One subsequent modification occurred in 1748 when free Christian Negroes, Indians, and mulattoes were allowed to appear in any case involving another Negro, Indian, or mulatto.[17] In brief, however, all these technicalities come down to the fact that the slaves normally could testify only in a capital case involving another Negro.

After 1732 the Negro possessed some fragments of that medieval remnant, benefit of clergy, to soften the harsh processes of justice under which he was often tried and convicted. This is not the place for a discussion of the long evolution of that institution from its origin as a means of protecting persons in clerical orders from trial in civil courts to the point that it saved all literate persons and finally virtually the entire population from certain punishments. To the Virginia Negro it was a means of escaping the prescribed punishment for his first commission of a good many capital crimes.[18] If his felony fell within benefit of clergy, the slave was burned in the hand to show that he had exhausted his use of the privilege. Then he received corporal punishment and was released.[19]

There is some question as to how early in the history of Virginia Negro slaves were able to claim benefit of clergy. Dalzell's study regards the 1732 law regulating the pleading of this privilege by Negroes as both the first regulation of benefit of clergy in the laws of the colony and the first occasion of its extension to slaves.[20] However, there was an earlier law in 1723

15. Ibid., 5: 127.
16. Ibid., 4: 326-27.
17. Ibid., 6: 107.
18. An excellent discussion is George W. Dalzell, *Benefit of Clergy in America & Related Matters* (Winston-Salem, N.C., 1955), Ch. X.
19. Hening, *Statutes*, 4: 326.
20. Dalzell, *Benefit of Clergy*, pp. 99, 104.

which placed insurrection or murder by a slave outside the privileges of benefit of clergy, an indication that Negroes might already have been clergyable.[21]

But Dalzell was probably entirely correct in thinking there was a considerable area of doubt about how far benefit of clergy extended to Negro slaves, and even to other Virginians. In particular the laws of England had not allowed women and persons who were illiterate to claim benefit of clergy until the reigns of William and Mary and Anne. It was not at all certain that these acts applied in the colonies to anyone. Moreover, the laws affecting the baptism of Negroes had not considered the possibility that conversion to Christianity conferred the right to benefit of clergy on slaves.

The 1732 legislation was the direct outgrowth of a case involving a Negro slave in which many of these doubts were combined. Mary Aggie, Virginia-born, Christianized, and the property of a Williamsburg widow, had committed a larceny for which she would have been clergyable in England, if a free woman. Governor Gooch interested himself in the case for some unexplained reason and after Mary Aggie's conviction by the Commission of Oyer and Terminer for York County, had an application for benefit of clergy entered in her behalf. The case was eventually considered by the Council and the General Court, and then submitted to England for a ruling. At that point all evidence of the outcome disappears, but then in 1732 the Virginia Assembly passed laws affecting benefit of clergy for women, illiterates, and slaves.[22]

Further definitions of benefit of clergy for slaves usually took the form of placing certain felonies outside the plea of clergy. Insurrection or murder fell beyond its scope in 1723.[23] Manslaughter, felonious breaking and entering, and thefts involving more than five shillings were exempted in 1724.[24] Then it was denied for a third conviction for hog stealing and for the malicious administration of poisonous medicines by the laws of

21. Hening, *Statutes*, 4: 126.
22. Mary Aggie's case is summarized in Dalzell, *Benefit of Clergy*, pp. 99-104; the 1732 statute is in Hening, *Statutes*, 4: 326.
23. Ibid., p. 126.
24. Ibid., p. 326.

1748.[25] So, in effect, so far as slaves were concerned the privilege of benefit of clergy began gradually to contract, except that in 1772 there was one redefinition of its applicability in cases of breaking and entering that favored the accused.[26]

Cases in which a Negro was on trial for a felony usually came to the courts with a minimum of delay.[27] The special commissions of oyer and a terminer helped speed the process, but efficiency was less at issue than the desire to impress other Negroes with the swift course of justice. In the long run a speedy trial was in the Negro's best interest, for slaves who did languish in jail awaiting trial sometimes paid a heavy penalty in physical suffering before they could begin to pay for their crime. In their 1762 session, for instance, the burgesses noted an allowance of £3:15:0 to a Caroline County man to compensate him for loss of thirty days' labor by a slave who had been frostbitten while confined. That same session allowed £80 to the owner of a slave who had lost both his legs and finally died from the frostbite he suffered in a cold jail.[28]

Peter Hansborough of Stafford County petitioned the Burgesses in an even worse case in 1771, but the delegates did not seem much disposed to compensate Hansborough for the death of his slave Sharper. The Negro had been charged with administering medicine illegally and was imprisoned to await examination by the justices. The weather turned so cold and rainy that, while Hansborough made his appearance at court, the justices declined to attend. Hansborough inquired after his slave and "found he was bitt by the Frost to Such a Degree that it Commanded Pity from every human heart." This was December, and the trial dragged on until May, when Sharper was acquitted. Hansborough related that he then "took the Poor distressed Slave home . . . [where he] . . . died."[29]

Just as the very nature of slave status had demanded trial procedures that to some extent abridged the traditional English

25. Ibid., 6: 105, 122-23.

26. Ibid., 8: 522-23.

27. Mays, *Edmund Pendleton*, 1: 45-46.

28. John P. Kennedy, ed. *Journals of the House of Burgesses of Virginia, 1761-1765* (Richmond, Va., 1907), pp. 71, 97, 102, 119.

29. *Virginia Magazine of History and Biography* 18 (Oct., 1910): 394-96.

and colonial guarantees of individual right, it just as logically required a system of punishment that was exclusively corporal. The courts might fine a master whose neglect contributed in some way to a criminal act of one of his Negroes, but the slave could not normally make satisfaction in this way. For minor offenses or when the slave was able to avail himself of benefit of clergy, whipping became the prescribed penalty—10 lashes for coming on a plantation without permission, 39 lashes for attending an unlawful meeting, or 39 for possessing weapons illegally, to cite a few examples.[30]

More serious crimes which did not warrant capital punishment, even in the harsh criminal codes of the day, required what may have been a more unpleasant fate than death itself. That penalty was multilation or dismemberment. A slave giving false evidence would, for instance, receive his 39 lashes and then have his ears nailed to the pillory for half an hour, after which they would be cut off.[31] Under the law of 1748 his ears would have been nailed to the pillory and then cut off one at a time rather than simultaneously.[32] Dismemberment was a favorite punishment for the slave who continually ran away, went abroad at night, or lay in hiding. Both the 1723 and 1748 acts specify its use for these offenses. Since the dismemberment usually took the form of cutting off a foot, it was a practical, if cruel way of curbing the sort of ungovernable Negro who really constituted the greatest threat of all against slavery as a police institution. That dismemberment sometimes reached proportions which struck even slaveowners as barbarous is, however, evidenced by a 1769 statute which in the future forbade the castration of a slave for continually lying out and reserved that punishment solely for Negroes guilty of the attempted rape of a white woman.[33]

Finally there were the whole series of crimes for which conviction carried the death penalty, the felonies for which

30. Hening, *Statutes*, 2: 481-82; 3: 179; 4: 126-34; etc. Corporal punishment of this sort could be ordered by a single justice in many instances. See Mays, *Edmund Pendleton*, 1: 45.

31. Hening, *Statutes*, 4: 127.

32. Ibid., 6: 106-7.

33. Ibid., 8: 358.

white persons would also have been executed plus offenses such as rebellion or the administering of medicines that applied only to slaves. According to the customary practice of colonial Virginia slaves were ordinarily hanged, but a slave named Eve who was convicted in Orange County of poisoning her master was drawn upon a hurdle to the place of execution and there burned at the stake.[34] Then there are also instances in which the head of a slave who had been hanged was cut off and put on public exhibition.

One economic problem arose with capital punishment of a slave. The owner was apt to view the execution as costing him the loss of a valuable piece of property, no matter how serious the slave's crime had been. In the 1705 statute affecting trial procedure for capital offenses, the justices were impowered to put a reasonable valuation upon any slave they condemned. When this valuation had been certified to the Assembly, the owner would be reimbursed from public funds.[35] This method of compensation remained in force throughout the colonial period with the result that few sessions of the Assembly fail to record favorable action on the request of some owner to be paid for an executed slave.[36]

The punishment which the courts meted out to slaves for crimes against public order in no way interfered with the disciplining of slaves by their owners and overseers. In fact, the law protected to extreme limits the master's privilege of punishing his slaves. One of the earliest pieces of legislation affecting slavery was the 1669 statute exempting a master from indictment for felony if a slave were killed while under punishment.[37] The law reasoned that there could be no felony without malicious intent and that no one could be presumed to destroy his own property deliberately and maliciously. The Assembly made some dent in this line of reasoning in 1723, by providing that the master might be indicted if there were at least one lawful witness to testify that the killing of the slave had been a willful

34. *Virginia Magazine,* 3 (Jan., 1896): 308-10.
35. Hening, *Statutes,* 3: 461.
36. A good example is *Virginia Magazine,* 18 (July, 1910): 282-83.
37. Hening, *Statutes,* 2: 270.

act.[38] But with this one unlikely exception owners remained exempt from prosecution for the death of a slave under correction, even though new royal governors were often instructed to work for laws to punish masters who deliberately killed or maimed a slave.

The dissection of a long list of laws is a tedious business at best; and once their contents have been outlined, there is not much more to be said. One significant development in the eighteenth century, however, was the collection of most of the criminal law affecting Negroes into the two comprehensive statutes of 1723 and 1748. They provided the colony with a "black code" nearly as well-defined and systematic as those of a later day.

This much can be said for the justice administered under these laws—it was often harsh, but it was uniform and not arbitrary. And it was rapid, for the slave did not often languish in jail awaiting trial. To that extent the slaves of colonial Virginia could have fared worse, as indeed they did in parts of the New World.

The net effect of these statutes, however, was to make the law for the Negro slave almost exclusively a police instrument for maintaining the stability of society and largely to demolish that more attractive side of law, the safeguarding of the individual from unnecessary invasions of his person. Perhaps only the uncomfortable fact that the slave was not fully a person in the eyes of the law saved this one-sidedness from seriously damaging, for free men even, the traditional guarantees to the individual that Virginia had inherited from English law.

2. The Incidence of Crime

The amount of legislative activity that went into the establishment of a criminal law for Negroes would imply a high rate of crime among slaves, but it is largely impossible either to substantiate or to disprove such an inference. The law may have been no more than an expression of the white man's fear of what could happen rather than what actually happened. There is simply not enough evidence to determine accurately

38. Ibid., 4: 132-33.

the amount of crime among slaves in the colonial period. Existing studies have quickly abandoned any such effort.[39]

Ordinarily the more serious crimes that came to trial by justices sitting under a special Commission of Oyer and Terminer were not particularly frequent. In the thirty-five year period from 1737 to 1772 Orange County had 25 such trials involving 31 Negroes. Chesterfield County from 1749 to 1774, a period of twenty-five years, witnessed 33 trials in which 44 Negroes were involved.[40]

There were more serious outbreaks of slave crime once in a while, when the trials of Negroes for felonies rose sharply. One of the best documented of these crime waves, which David J. Mays has described quite fully, swept through Caroline County in the three or four years at the end of the French and Indian War.[41] In a matter of relatively few months no less than 12 Negroes went on trial for various felonies, including murder, the illegal administration of medicine, and arson. Nine of the twelve were convicted and executed, two were allowed to plead benefit of clergy, and one won acquittal.[42]

Next to his consuming dread of an organized slave rising the average white planter most feared an individual act of violence by one of his slaves. Poisoning seemed to occupy a special niche in his chamber of horrors. There were just enough instances of masters who had been killed by a slave in this way to lend a certain amount of justification to the white's perpetual sense of insecurity. In an age when no one could accuse the press of sensationalism a colonial printer never missed an opportunity to report the poisoning of a master or overseer.[43]

The instances in which slaves were made to suffer some indignity beyond the normal execution by hanging were usually punishments for the murder of the Negro's master. The slave Eve who was burned at the stake in Orange County had

39. See, for example, Arthur P. Scott, *Criminal Law in Colonial Virginia* (Chicago, 1930), p. 311.
40. Ibid., p. 312.
41. Mays, *Edmund Pendleton*, 1: 41.
42. Ibid., pp. 42-44.
43. *Georgia Gazette*, March 30, 1768, which contains an account of a multiple poisoning in Alexandria, Virginia.

poisoned her owner.[44] Most of the instances in which executed Negroes were to have their heads cut off and publicly displayed involved crimes of arson or poisoning.[45]

Since the courts did not often deal with petty crimes committed by slaves, it is even more difficult to say anything about such misdemeanors than about felonies which came to trial. The theft of a small article, a fight between two of the slaves, or some similar misdeed could be punished by the master without bringing the matter to the county court.[46]

Information about Negro crime in Williamsburg is as sketchy as that for the rest of the colony. There are enough newspaper accounts to assure that there were criminals among the slaves who lived here, if any such assurance were needed. And the range of their misdeeds seems about what it was everywhere else. If anything, there is a strong suggestion that, just as the slaves of the capital were among the most skilled in the entire colony, they also made the most artful criminals.

The annals of identifiable slave crimes in Williamsburg begin with a mulatto slave, Sarah, the property of Archibald Blair, who received a death sentence in 1728 for setting a house on fire.[47] Another account of an equally grave felony concerns an attempted poisoning which was reported in the *Maryland Gazette:*

WILLIAMSBURG. May 20, A Negro Boy in this City, set on by a Couple of Negro Fellows, went in his Mistress's Name to a Shop for some Arsenick to Poison Rats, and got a little; but took the Opportunity, when some Milk and Rice was on the Fire, to drop the Whole amongst it, unperceived: All the Family, consisting of nine or ten Persons, eat of it at Dinner, and in a few Minutes after were taken with a violent Vomiting; which created a Suspicion of Poison being the Occasion, Physicians were immediately called, who ordered them what is necessary in those Cases, and it is hoped are now out of Danger. All the Negroes are taken up and committed to Prison, and

44. *Virginia Magazine,* 3 (Jan., 1896): 308.
45. Ibid., 16 (July, 1908): 95.
46. Scott, *Criminal Law in Virginia,* p. 311.
47. York County Records, Orders and Wills, Book 16, p. 511.

it is hoped will be made Examples of, to deter others from such Villainy.[48]

Robbery appears to have been more common. A great many of the runaways from Williamsburg were Negroes who had fled after committing some theft.[49] John Greenhow observed of one of his runaways, a cooper named Harry, "He is a sly thief, few locks or doors will turn him, and is seldom long in a place before he puts his ingenuity in practice."[50] One instance of stealing by a free Negro is that of Charles Oats who broke into a cellar and took a chest of clothes and £50 cash.[51] Oats confessed, delivered up the money and part of the clothes, but then escaped. A slave named Moody was suspected in 1772 of having broken open an outhouse of Lord Dunmore's and made off with 19 turkeys belonging to the governor.[52] This was not the end of trouble for Moody, for the next year Benjamin Bucktrout advertised the slave's latest round of crimes:

Run away a Negro Fellow, named *Moody,* a notorious Villain, who has been tried three Times at *York* Court, about three Weeks ago he received a very serious Whipping for knocking out a Negro's Eye, and last *Sunday* robbed a white Man of twenty Shillings, and a Silk Handkerchief. This is to forewarn all Persons from harbouring or employing him on any Account.[53]

John Greenhow seems to have had more than his share of difficulties over the crimes of his slaves. Harry, the sly lock-picker, was an easy case compared with two other of his Negroes, Fay and Emanuel. The first of the pair had beaten his overseer, and Emanuel had fought with Greenhow himself, throwing his master to the ground. The two, whom Greenhow termed notorious thieves, then made their escape.[54]

48. June 9, 1763.
49. *Virginia Gazette,* March 20, 1752.
50. Ibid., (Purdie), April 11, 1766.
51. Ibid., (Purdie), August 16, 1776.
52. Ibid., (Rind), March 26, 1772.
53. Ibid., (Purdie and Dixon), September 23, 1773.
54. Ibid., (Purdie), January 17, 1777.

3. The Fugitive Slaves

Much of the crime committed by Negro slaves was to some degree one possible means of resisting the demands of slavery. It was, to be sure, a fairly desperate method, particularly if a slave resorted to anything so extreme as the murder of his master and so insured his own execution. There was a much safer way of refusing to accept bondage. That was simply to run away at the first opportunity. The chances of being retaken were good, but not good enough to deter great numbers of slaves from becoming fugitives.

For a slave to run away was as much a criminal act as for one to rob or kill. The owner did not have to rely solely on his own resources to recapture his man. He could count upon the machinery of law to assist him. The fugitive slave represented in a number of ways, however, a distinct problem from the ordinary slave criminal. His offense was too common to treat it as a felony, until it became habitual.[55] Ordinarily he stood convicted by his very act of flight; therefore provision for trial and punishment by the courts were largely unnecessary. Swift recapture and return to his owner were the basic needs, and these the law tried to provide. Punishment by whipping could be administered by the officials responsible for his return without a court decree.

Before the advent of slavery in a legal sense Negroes were dealt with under the laws that applied to all runaway indentured servants, white or black. These enactments required fugitives to serve extra time, usually twice the length of their absence, as compensation to the master for the loss of their labor.[56] It was, in fact, a revision of these laws that constituted the first legal recognition in Virginia that the status of the

55. For slaves who became habitual runaways or remained in hiding committing various depredations—"lying out" as the eighteenth century expressed it—more drastic legal procedures evolved. Two justices of the peace could issue a proclamation permitting such offenders to be killed without quarter. The sheriff could collect a force to hunt them down, or an individual captor might collect a reward for killing a Negro outlawed in this manner. If an "outlying" slave were taken alive, he was not executed, however, but punished by dismemberment. Hening, *Statutes,* 3: 86, 210-11, 460-61; 4: 32; 6: 110-11; 8: 358, 522-23.

56. Ibid., 1: 254-55, 401, 440.

Negro was changing so that he could be held as a servant for life. This occurred in the statute of 1661/62 which referred specifically to "negroes who are incapable of making satisfaction by addition of time."[57]

Not much later, in 1669, a system by which recaptured servants were to be returned to their masters was defined by law. A fugitive who was retaken was carried before the nearest justice in order to determine the name of his master. Then the man was to be delivered from constable to constable along the route to his home.[58] The next year the law was modified to instruct each constable to give the fugitive a severe whipping as he passed through his jurisdiction, and at the same time runaway Negroes were specifically stated to be comprehended in these acts.[59] A reward was also established for recapturing a runaway—1,000 pounds of tobacco in 1669 but reduced in 1670 to a less attractive 200 pounds with much more stringent inquiry into the claimant's right to collect.[60]

After slavery was fully established, these arrangements, that is, the reward of 200 pounds of tobacco and the system of returning runaways through successive constables remained in force with only minor variations. Thus the 1705 law, while largely repeating existing regulations, did omit the requirement that every constable through whom a man was returned should administer a whipping.[61] Now only the first constable gave his thirty-nine lashes; so a hapless fugitive might have gotten home with at least a little skin on his back.

The 1705 law also introduced another modification in which the Public Gaol at Williamsburg figured prominently. Before it had been more or less assumed that the recaptured man would identify the name and residence of his owner. The Assembly overlooked the growing number of Negroes, some of whom knew no English and could not give this information and others of whom pretended to be new and feigned a lack of understanding of English. Now, when it was impossible to identify

57. Ibid., 2: 116-17.
58. Ibid., pp. 273-74.
59. Ibid., pp. 277-79.
60. Ibid., pp. 283-84.
61. Ibid., 3: 456-57.

the owner, a slave was to be brought down to Williamsburg to the Public Gaol of the colony.[62] Eventually it became permissible to sell Negroes unclaimed after a reasonable time. With the founding of a newspaper in Williamsburg, it also became possible for the jailer to advertise runaways he was holding.

Justices and constables immediately began to send unidentified runaways to the capital, at times in such haste that a slave taken only a few miles from his home plantation might well be sent a long distance to Williamsburg before anyone had a chance to identify him. So, after 1726, it was necessary to hold a Negro first for two months in the jail of the county where he had been captured. Then if he had not been claimed, the constable would pass him along through the other constables to the Public Gaol.[63] The volume of Negroes brought to Williamsburg under these laws was considerable, for the columns of the *Virginia Gazette* carried a more or less steady flow of advertisements.[64] Such runaways may have furnished an addition to the local labor force, since they could be hired out under proper safeguards. Not many of the unidentified ones were sold here, since the court of the county in which they had first been captured had this authority.

In 1748, the same year in which the main body of criminal law affecting Negroes was overhauled and consolidated, an attempt was made to do the same thing regarding runaways in an act on servants and slaves.[65] This latter enactment, however, failed to include a suspending clause, holding up its effective date until it had received the royal assent. For this reason Virginians received notice in 1752 that it had been disallowed, but the Assembly moved quickly to pass a similar law in the proper form in 1753.[66] It was essentially a restatement of the law as it had stood since 1726.

In the 1760s there was a final attempt to alter the means of handling captured fugitives. An act of 1765 provided for a

62. Ibid., p. 456.
63. Ibid., 4: 168-75.
64. See, for example, *Virginia Gazette*, September 15, 1737; September 22, 1738; March 21, 1745; January 2, 1752.
65. Hening, *Statutes*, 5: 547-48.
66. Ibid., 6: 356-69.

captor who had determined the owner of a fugitive to carry the man before the justice of the peace of the county. Then the captor was to take the responsibility of returning the runaway to the master upon himself, for which he was entitled to payment of 5 shillings plus 4 pence a mile.[67] This method, while eliminating the use of the constables except for slaves whose masters could not be determined, had obvious shortcomings. It is no surprise to find the law altered four years later in 1769 on the ground that it had been ineffective. Now a captor could follow the procedure of 1765, receiving larger sums of 10 shillings plus 6 pence a mile; or he could simply take the runaway to the county jail, where the older arrangements that still applied to slaves of unidentified masters could be followed.[68]

The conclusion is inescapable that the volume of runaway slaves was large, large enough to sap a part of the economic advantage of a slave labor force. The small stereotype of a black figure hurrying along with a parcel of clothing tied on a stick and slung across his shoulder identified listings of fugitives in substantially every issue of the *Gazette*. From George Washington to the humblest master few owners escaped the loss of Negroes in this way.[69]

The ease with which the slave community in Williamsburg hid fugitives must suggest that the capital was no more immune from runaways than anywhere else in the colony and that recapturing them was no easier. Williamsburg's share of the *Gazette* advertisements was large, and not even the printers themselves escaped the disagreeable necessity of using their own columns to attempt to recover a slave.[70]

Not all of these escaped slaves had an idea of achieving permanent freedom. Free soil did not yet exist to the north. If a slave really intended to live as a free man, the possibilities were limited and, in some cases, the hardships almost as unendurable as slavery itself. He had essentially two alternatives. He might

67. Ibid., 8: 135-37.
68. Ibid., pp. 358-61.
69. *The Negro in Virginia*. Compiled by the Writers' Program of the Work Projects Administration (New York, 1940), p. 128.
70. *Virginia Gazette* (Purdie and Dixon), November 24, 1768; (Dixon and Hunter), January 28, 1775; (Purdie), March 8, 1776.

make his way to one of the hidden, illegal communities of refugee Negroes on the western frontier of Virginia or in the Dismal Swamp. Otherwise and with less risk, if he were a skilled craftsman or light-skinned, he might get to a settled community where he could pass without too many questions as a free Negro. For Virginia slaves in the eighteenth century North Carolina offered the best opportunity for this latter course.

Bob, a slave of the Williamsburg innkeeper William Trebell, is a good illustration.[71] Bob, a man of 26 described as having been "burnt when young, by which he has a scar on the wrist of his right hand, the thumb of his left hand burnt off, and the hand [turned] in," escaped on a Saturday night in April of 1767. It is his past which was, however, more relevant. Bob had just been brought back from Hertford County in North Carolina after being away eight years. Part of the time he had lived in Charleston, South Carolina. Then for the last three years he had lived in North Carolina under the name of Edward or Edmund Tamar, had married, and with the protection of a man named Van Pelt had passed as a freeman. The fact that he could read and write and was an able carpenter and tailor had certainly made his deception easier. Some of the Negro women in Williamsburg were also able to get away in the hope of passing as free, including Nanny, "a brisk genteel sensible wench," whom her owner, Jane Vobe, suspected of having gone off with the New American Company of actors.[72]

Very frequently runaway slaves were less concerned about a permanent escape than simply returning to a locale from which they had recently been purchased or moved. John Maclean, for instance, bought a slave girl, Judith, and her year-old child at the sale of slaves from Middlesex County held on April 30, 1773, at Williamsburg. The following day she slipped off and was advertised as having probably started back to her Middlesex master.[73] Another girl, only 14 or 15 years old, from this same lot of slaves escaped in October, presumably to return to

71. Ibid. (Purdie and Dixon), April 16, 1767. See also the advertisement by James Southall for his slave, Peter, ibid., (Purdie and Dixon), January 8, 1767.

72. Ibid., (Purdie and Dixon), June 30, 1768.

73. Ibid., (Purdie and Dixon), May 6, 1773.

her mother, who was still a cook for the planter who had sold the daughter.[74] John, "6 feet high, 17 years old, well grown, with remarkable long feet," was known to have returned from Williamsburg to Warwick, where he had a father and some other relatives.[75] Often the attraction of the slave's former residence was the fact that a wife or husband was still living there, as in the case of Peter, the property of John Fox of Williamsburg, who for this reason had returned to Gloucester County.[76] Running away for the sake of returning to a familiar location or rejoining relatives was a two-way street so far as Williamsburg was concerned; for there were also slaves who escaped into town after being sold or leased elsewhere. One instance of this is the case of Billy, a 20-year old slave advertised by his master in Amherst County as a runaway and suspected of having gone back to Williamsburg, since he had grown up and been trained as a shoemaker there.[77] In a number of instances slaves who had accompanied masters to Williamsburg took advantage of the busy atmosphere of the capital to make an escape.[78]

After a time it becomes distinctly noticeable how many runaway Negroes were drawn from the more highly skilled classes of labor. A high proportion seemed to be craftsmen, and some were able to read and write. The average runaway often seemed to be a slave like Johnny, a mulatto serving man, able to read and write, and once the property of Peyton Randolph, who escaped from Edmund Randolph in late 1777.[79]

It cannot be overlooked, however, that many runaway slaves were simply ordinary field hands, quite often so recently imported that they knew no English. This was more characteristic of the early eighteenth century and of other areas than Williamsburg, although most of the recaptured slaves brought into the Public Gaol, because their masters were unidentified,

74. Ibid., (Purdie and Dixon), January 27, 1774.
75. Ibid., (Purdie), July 25, 1777.
76. Ibid., (Purdie), October 17, 1777.
77. Ibid., (Clarkson and Davis), October 30, 1779.
78. Ibid., (Purdie and Dixon), March 31, 1768; June 29, 1769; November 14, 1771.
79. Ibid., (Purdie), December 12, 1777.

were "new Negroes."[80] There was one occasion when a group of fourteen recently imported Negroes fled in a body from a Hanover County merchant, John Burnley, who was probably holding them for sale.[81]

In the final analysis these runaways were perhaps a mixed lot, as mixed as their motives for escape. Some had genuine hopes of freedom, and a very few made good on them. Some fled from sheer desperation, not caring any longer about the risk of recapture. Others were more temporary absentees than real fugitives, seeking only a brief return to relatives from whom they had been separated. Whatever the reasons, the number of slaves who, in the eighteenth century use of the word, "eloped" is a powerful argument that few Negroes accepted the demands of slavery complacently.

4. The Threat of Rebellion

There has already been occasion, in connection with the movement for high import duties on slaves, to comment on the lurking fear of insurrection which haunted every slaveowner. As the number of slaves mounted steadily toward half the population of the colony—and, of course, more than half in areas where the slaves were really concentrated—it became possible to conceive of the destruction of society itself, if a Negro uprising were really to take hold. Newspapers all over the colonies were quick to publish every available detail of a real or rumored attempt of slaves to rebel; and much of the restrictive legislation against Negroes in the colony was admittedly aimed at this unwelcome possibility.[82]

80. Ibid., September 2, 1737; September 15, 1737; September 28, 1738; January 2, 1752; (Purdie and Dixon), July 8, 1773; February 3, 1774; June 16, 1774; August 4, 1774.

81. Ibid., (Purdie and Dixon), August 19, 1773. Two months later Burnley had recovered ten of the Negroes, but the others were still in hiding near West Point, ibid., (Purdie and Dixon), October 28, 1773.

82. The pertinent Virginia laws are those of 1680, 1682, 1723, and 1748. See above, section 1 of this chapter. Gerald W. Mullin, *Flight and Rebellion: Slave Resistance in Eighteenth-Century Virginia* (New York, 1971), *passim*, is extremely important for the study of slave rebellions and other forms of resistance. Mullin also thinks the whites were less apprehensive and insecure than I have described.

To what extent was the alarm of the whites exaggerated? One count of uprisings or threats of uprisings during the entire course of slavery in Virginia lists 72 of which only 9 occurred before 1776.[83] The truth is difficult to measure; for instead of specific, brief episodes more often there were periods of general unrest lasting several years at a time. Judged on this basis, about a fourth of the years from 1700 to 1775 were marred by an abnormal degree of this uneasiness. The fact remains, however, that no white person was killed in an organized slave insurrection in Virginia before the Nat Turner rising of 1831.

The first recorded attempt at a slave uprising in Virginia occurred in the Northern Neck in 1687. As so often happened, one of the men involved confessed and the attempt was checked. The slave who had been leader was not executed but was whipped around Jamestown from the prison to the gallows and back, forced to wear an iron collar for the rest of his life, and forbidden ever to leave his master's plantation.[84]

A more serious plot, which centered in Surry and Isle of Wight Counties but also involved James City, was uncovered in March, 1709.[85] Once again it was a slave who betrayed the plan to the whites—a Negro named Will, the property of Robert Ruffin of Surry.[86] It fell to the Council to direct an investigation of the whole matter and issue instructions for the trial and punishment of the Negroes involved. The way in which they proceeded provides a good picture of the operation of all levels of government in the colony in the face of what, to these men, presented a serious crisis. First of all, the Council apparently issued warrants for the arrest of all suspects, similar to one issued for four Negroes in Bruton Parish, Angola Peter, Bumbara Peter, Mingo, and Robin.[87] Then the county justices of Surry and Isle of Wight were ordered to examine all suspected slaves, releasing those only slightly involved with

83. *Negro in Virginia*, p. 175.

84. Ibid., p. 174; "Randolph Manuscript," *Virginia Magazine,* 19 (April, 1911): 151.

85. H. R. McIlwaine and Wilmer L. Hall, eds. *Executive Journals of the Council of Colonial Virginia* (Richmond, Va., 1925-1945), 3: 234-35.

86. *Journals of the House of Burgesses, 1702-1712,* p. 270.

87. *Virginia Magazine,* 17 (Jan., 1909): 34.

appropriate punishment and holding the leaders in the county jail, until the record of their examination could be examined by the president of the Council, Edmund Jenings.[88] James City Negroes were not considered to be so deeply involved. Here, with a single exception, the slaves, who had been rounded up and held under guard, were to be tried at the next county court, punished, and released.[89] There is an account of the close cross-examination of several of these slaves in a letter from Philip Ludwell to Jenings. The questioning by Ludwell and three others had cleared Commissary Blair's slaves and a number of others of complicity, but it had also turned up the evidence against John Brodnax's Jamy, the one James City slave ordered held in prison.[90]

About a month later the Council ordered the principal culprits, those still held in jail, to be tried before the General Court, where three of them were presumably convicted and hanged. One of the "chief Actors," Peter, belonging to Samuel Thompson of Surry, had escaped, and a reward of £10 alive or £5 dead was offered for his recapture.[91]

The episode had a happier ending for Robert Ruffin's Will. After he had given away the insurrection, it became necessary to move him to the Northern Neck because some of the other Negroes threatened his life. Then at its meeting in the fall of 1710 the Assembly voted him his freedom as a reward for his service to the colony, the occasion being marred only by the complaint of his former master, Ruffin, that the £40 voted by the Assembly was less than he had been offered for the Negro by a prospective buyer.[92]

Another plan for an uprising was headed off in 1722, prompting Governor Drysdale to include in his first message to the assembly a request for improving the militia and for passing

88. *Executive Journals of Colonial Virginia*, 3: 234-35.

89. Ibid., 3, p. 235.

90. *Virginia Magazine*, 19 (January, 1911), 23-24.

91. *Executive Journals of Colonial Virginia*, 3: 236; *Negro in Virginia*, p. 174.

92. *Journals of the House of Burgesses, 1702-1712*, 270, 276, 282, 284, 288, 292, 298; Hening, *Statutes*, 3: 537-38.

stricter laws as a protection against Negroes.[93] The slave code was, in fact, strengthened that year.[94]

The years of 1729 and 1730 seem to have brought a relatively longer period of unrest among slaves which may have continued through most of the decade of the 30s.[95] The first incident occurred in June of 1729 on a new plantation near the head of the James River. There a group of about fifteen Negroes seized arms, provisions, and tools and made off for the mountains. The search party found them already settled in a secluded area, where they had even begun to clear ground for crops. A brief exchange of gunfire brought about the surrender of the slaves, however, and their small colony was destroyed.[96]

There was more trouble the next year, touched off by a rumor that former Governor Spotswood, just back from England, had brought an order from the Crown to free all Christian slaves. This was more a matter of general unrest than a concerted plot. The governor, at the time Gooch, reported that by "keeping the Militia to their Duty, by Imprisonment and severe whipping of the most Suspected, this Disturbance was very soon Quashed, and until about six weeks afterwards we were easy . . ."[97] Then there was more trouble. About two hundred slaves in Norfolk and Princess Anne counties gathered on a Sunday at church time and elected officers to lead an intended rebellion. In this instance four of the Negroes involved were executed.[98] A certain amount of continuing uneasiness is reflected in Gooch's address to the assembly in 1736, in which he recommended strengthening the militia as a means of policing the slaves; in his proclamation of October 29, 1736, on the same subject; and in the 1738 revision of the law requesting the militia to include

93. Ibid., *1712-1726*, p. 360.
94. Ibid, *1712-1726*, p. 395.
95. *Executive Journals of Colonial Virginia*, 4: 462-63.
96. *Virginia Magazine*, 28 (Oct., 1920): 299-300.
97. Ibid., 32 (Oct., 1924): 322-23. Also, see above, p. 70 for the relation between this unrest and Anglican missionary efforts among the Virginia Negroes.
98. Ibid.

a system of four-men patrols to police slave quarters and suspected gathering places of Negroes in every county.[99]

Another unsettled period occurred in and near Williamsburg during the 1770s. The number of runaways advertised seemed noticeably large, and accounts of trouble with slaves in York, James City, and Hanover counties circulated in newspapers as far away as New York.[100] This was in part responsible for the establishment of a night watch in Williamsburg in 1772 to consist of four people to patrol the streets, cry the hours, and "use their best Endeavours to preserve Peace and good Order, by apprehending and bringing to Justice Hall disorderly People, Slaves as well as others."[101] About the same time there was a strict patrol in Yorktown, and Negroes found on the street were picked up and held overnight.[102]

For suppression of an incipient revolt the colony relied largely on the county militia and, after 1738, the system of patrols, reinforced by such local activity as the Williamsburg night watch. From what we know about the colonial militia, it is not likely that these men were over-diligent, until there was an indication of trouble. Still, the colony proved able to act swiftly in an emergency. Real emergencies, however, were relatively infrequent; for well-laid plots by slaves were much rarer in eighteenth-century Virginia than what could be more correctly described as periods of unusual restiveness.

99. *Journals of the House of Burgesses, 1727-1740*, p. 243; *Executive Journals of Colonial Virginia*, 4: 383, 470-71; Hening, *Statutes*, 5: 19, 24.

100. *Maryland Gazette*, February 8, 1770; *New York Journal or General Advertiser*, February 15, 1770.

101. *Virginia Gazette* (Purdie and Dixon), July 16, 1772.

102. Ibid., (Pinkney), August 10, 1775.

CHAPTER XI

The Impact of the Revolution

UNTIL the American Revolution deepened into a struggle expressed partly in terms of establishing human liberty, it occurred to few Virginians—or for that matter to few of the colonists anywhere—to question the existence of chattel slavery on moral grounds. The long attempt to discourage new importations of Negroes, once regarded as based on such objections, has been found to have its real roots in social and economic considerations and to stress control, not prohibition, of the slave trade. The humanitarian effort to Christianize and educate the Negro obviously rested upon a moral awareness of sorts, but it viewed slavery as either actually or potentially a civilizing institution and therefore productive of good.

Undoubtedly a relatively large number of people sensed a certain evil about slavery. Their favorite line of reasoning was that it degraded master and bondsman alike. If anything, they asserted, the owner paid the greater price, because he was encouraged in idleness and profligacy by his human wealth.[1] This was a sentiment which arose more out of a sense of frustration than a desire for action. Indeed most of its adherents would have condemned any wholesale attack on slavery as a hopeless complication of an already touchy problem. Moreover, few of these people really believed the Negro possessed the degree of humanity requisite for life in a free society.

New arrivals in the colony, having had no chance to accustom themselves gradually to the idea of living in daily contact with slavery, sometimes were in for a shock. Robert Beverley, soon after reaching Virginia, wrote to Edward Athawes that he felt "an Aversion to Slavery; 'tis something so very contradictory to Humanity, that I am really ashamed of my Country whenever I consider of it; & if ever I bid adieu to Virginia, it will be from that Cause alone . . ."[2] Something of

1. *Virginia Gazette*, April 10, 1752.
2. Robert Beverley to Edward Athawes, July 11, 1761, in Robert Beverley Letterbook, Manuscript Division, Library of Congress.

the same sense of revulsion is apparent in Governor Fauquier's will:

It is now expedient that I should dispose of my slaves, a part of my estate in its nature disagreeable to me, but which my situation made necessary for me; the disposal of which has constantly given me uneasiness whenever the thought occurred to me. I hope I shall be found to have been a merciful Master to them and that no one of them will rise up in judgment against me in that Great Day when all my actions will be exposed to Public view., For with what face can I expect mercy from an offended God, if I have not myself shewn mercy to these dependant on me. But it is not sufficient that I have been this Master in my life, I must provide for them at my death, by using my utmost endeavors that they experience as little misery during their lives as their very unhappy and pitiable condition will allow.[3]

Fauquier then went on to stipulate that the slaves in his estate be allowed to choose their new master within six months and that a new owner so designated should have the right to purchase them at a quarter below the market price. Children were also not to be separated from their mothers. Those who were not purchased under these conditions could then be purchased by the executors and after that sold in the regular way. The extant records of the executors do not make it clear to what extent the governor's wishes were followed, but the slaves were sold here in Williamsburg.

Concrete proposals that slavery in the colony be abolished were rare, ineffective, and certainly unrepresentative of the prevailing climate of opinion. There was a curious letter signed with the pseudonym, Philo-Bombastia, which appeared in the *Virginia Gazette* in 1752 and advocated full religious toleration, the admission of all foreigners, and the freeing of the Negroes in order to make Virginia a land of liberty and moderation rivaling Pennsylvania.[4] About the only organized antislavery movement in Virginia before independence was that of the small Quaker remnant. One of its leaders, Robert

3. York County Records, Wills and Inventories, Book 21, pp. 397-403.
4. *Virginia Gazette*, March 20, 1752.

Pleasants of Henrico County corresponded widely with anti-slavery men elsewhere, made some efforts to influence the General Assembly against slavery in the 1770s and seems to have attempted individual acts of manumission in violation of the existing laws.[5] The Cedar Creek Meeting in Hanover County became another center of Quaker resistance to slavery.[6]

It was difficult to conceive of outright abolition, however, when even a private act of manumission continued to be nearly impossible. The 1691 law prohibiting the freeing of a Negro unless voted by the assembly in recognition of some meritorious deed or unless the slave were transported out of the colony by his owner continued in effect, reinforced by a similar act in 1723.[7] From time to time the assembly used its power to free a slave by law, but always sparingly.[8] From the will of Philip Ludwell, dated February 28, 1767, it would also seem that an occasional owner met the burdensome demand of taking a slave from the colony in order to manumit him.[9] Ludwell provided that two girls, Jane and Sarah, could be carried to England and there set free in order to fulfill a promise to Cress, the mother of the girls, who had been a faithful nurse to Ludwell's own children.

The years of political controversy with Great Britain which preceded the outbreak of actual war had the net effect, so far as the position of the Negro was concerned, of reopening the old question of importing new blacks. It became possible now to oppose the trade as one more part of the economic weapon of nonimportation. Thus the 1769 Association contained an article pledging those who signed not to buy Negroes who had not been on the continent at least a year.[10] The burgesses in the

5. Adair P. Archer, "The Quaker's Attitude Towards the Revolution," *William and Mary Quarterly*, 2nd ser., 1 (July, 1921): 168; "Letters of Robert Pleasants of Curles," ibid., (April, 1921), p. 109; ibid., (October, 1922), pp. 274-75.

6. Mrs. Douglas Summers Brown, "Cedar Creek Monthly Meeting and Its Meeting House," ibid., 2nd ser., 19 (July, 1939): 293.

7. William Waller Hening, ed., *The Statutes at Large Being a Collection of all the Laws of Virginia* (Richmond, Va., etc., 1810-1823), 3: 87-88; 4: 132.

8. Ibid., 3: 537-38.

9. *Virginia Magazine of History and Biography*, 32 (July, 1924): 288.

10. *Journals of the House of Burgesses, 1766-1769*, p. xli.

spring of 1771 unsuccessfully addressed the governor with a request that he approve legislation which would close the slave trade.[11] The Virginia Convention which met in the fall of 1774 agreed not to allow the overseas slave trade to continue.[12] Although some of the protests were stated to rest on a desire to end "a Wicked, Cruel & unnatural Trade," the motivation of the colonial leaders was much more the same blend of fear of civil disorder and damage to the economy that had now prevailed for virtually a whole century.[13]

The wave of shocked disbelief and bitter anger that greeted Lord Dunmore's offer in 1775 to free slaves who joined him is proof enough that the leaders of the Virginia Patriots had not yet brought themselves to the point of considering emancipation. The circumstances of the governor's move, which did more than anything else to render him hateful in the eyes of the colony, are familiar. Claiming to have been driven from Williamsburg as an aftermath of the removal of the powder from the Public Magazine in April, 1775, Dunmore had moved by stages to the harbor of Norfolk, where under the protection of his ships, he was maintaining a shadowy government.

Finally, one of his desperation moves was a proclamation of November 7, 1775, offering among other things to free any servants or Negro slaves who would come in to his side and bear arms against the rebellious colonists.[14] The combination of arms and freedom for slaves sent a sickening fear through the Virginians, who saw in Dunmore's "Damned, infernal, Diabolical proclamation" not so much the potential defeat of their own political effort as the undermining of society itself.[15]

Although there were a number of derisive comments, such as

11. *Ibid., 1770-1772,* pp. 283-84.

12. *Virginia Gazette* (Purdie and Dixon), August 11, 1774.

13. *Virginia Magazine,* 18 (April, 1910): 166-67.

14. Francis L. Berkeley, Jr., *Dunmore's Proclamation of Emancipation* (Charlottesville, Va., 1941), *frontispiece;* Benjamin Quarles, "Lord Dunmore As Liberator," *William and Mary Quarterly,* 3rd ser., 15 (Oct. 1958): 494-507.

15. John Hatley Norton to John Norton, [October 16, 1775?] in Francis Hatley Norton, ed., *John Norton & Sons Merchants of London and Virginia* (Richmond, Va., 1937), pp. 391-92; *Virginia Magazine,* 14 (Jan., 1907): 253.

the account in Purdie's *Gazette* of the formidable, eighty-man *"Royal Regiment of Black Fusiliers"* marching to the martial tune of *"Hungry Niger, parch'd Corn!"* Virginians were inclined, if anything to become unreasonable in their fear.[16] However, Dunmore's move was one of desperation, and the danger was not really so great. The militia organization was then about as effective as it would be during the entire war, and events had already been set in motion which led to the decisive defeat of the Loyalists suffered at Great Bridge the following month. The Virginia Convention hastened to provide the death penalty for slaves recaptured from Dunmore, though it offered to pardon those who left him voluntarily, and various writers to the *Virginia Gazette* began to counter Dunmore's appeal.[17]

Still, Dunmore's offer of freedom filtered through to slaves in a great many places, and a certain number of them tried to reach the British base at Norfolk.[18] Some were already there who had escaped before the formal proclamation, been seized by British raiding parties, or been brought in by Loyalist masters.[19] Rumors around Williamsburg placed the number of former slaves with Dunmore as high as two thousand, but the Negro troops actually under arms at the Battle of Great Bridge numbered about three or four hundred. In all, some eight hundred Negroes perhaps reached Dunmore.[20]

Dunmore's defeat at Great Bridge and the subsequent evacuation of Norfolk reduced him more to the status of a nuisance than a real menace, although he was to continue to harass the coast for several months. His ships carried a number of the Negroes along, and all through the spring of 1776 there contin-

16. *Virginia Gazette* (Purdie), March 22, 1776.

17. *The Proceedings of the Convention of Delegates Held at the Town of Richmond . . . on Friday, the 1st of December, 1775* (Richmond, Va., 1816), p. 66; *Virginia Gazette* (Purdie), November 17, 1765; (Dixon and Hunter), November 25, December 16, 1775.

18. Ibid., (Purdie), January 26, 1776.

19. David J. Mays, *Edmund Pendleton, 1721-1803: A Biography* (Cambridge, Mass., 1952), 2: 56; *Virginia Gazette* (Dixon and Hunter), October 28, 1775; *Virginia Magazine,* 17 (April, 1909): 167-68.

20. *Virginia Gazette* (Dixon and Hunter), December 2, 1775; Quarles, "Lord Dunmore as Liberator," p. 506.

ued to be slaves who slipped off, sometimes in a stolen boat or canoe, to join Dunmore.[21] In a number of cases they were intercepted by the Patriots and returned to their owners, sold at auction, or occasionally executed.[22] A worse fate awaited many of those who actually reached the British; for both on their ships and at Dunmore's last headquarters on Gwynn's Island fever and smallpox took a horrible toll.[23]

For that matter the unrest promoted by the war kept the Negro population stirred up all through the next several years. Whenever the British were operating in Virginia, there were always a certain number of Negroes who escaped to the enemy or were captured on coastal raids.[24] Others simply ran off into hiding; the figures for fugitives remained unusually high throughout the Revolution. Jefferson estimated 30,000 in the one year of 1778.[25]

There were also Negro troops fighting on the Patriot side, perhaps about five thousand during the course of the war. Largely at Washington's insistence, Negroes were at first excluded from Continental enlistments by orders of July 9 and November 12, 1775. Concern about the effect of Dunmore's proclamation, however, quickly persuaded the American commander to change his mind; and from December 1, 1775, free Negroes were accepted in the Continental Army.[26] The majority of Negro troops thereafter enlisted came from the northern colonies, and, with the exception of two special companies from Rhode Island and Connecticut, they were scattered through existing regiments.[27]

21. *Virginia Gazette* (Dixon and Hunter), February 3, 1776.

22. Ibid., (Purdie), March 29, 1776; (Dixon and Hunter), April 13, 1776.

23. Ibid., (Purdie), March 8, 1776; (Dixon and Hunter), June 15, July 20, 1776.

24. Ibid., (Purdie), September 19, November 28, 1777; "Diary of Landon Carter," *William and Mary Quarterly*, 1st ser., 20 (Jan., 1912): 176, 178-79, 182-83, 185.

25. John Hope Franklin, *From Slavery to Freedom: A History of American Negroes* (New York, 1948), p. 133.

26. Franklin, *Slavery to Freedom*, pp. 131-33. The most recent full-scale treatment of the Negro in the Revolution is Benjamin Quarles, *The Negro in the American Revolution* (Chapel Hill, 1961).

27. Franklin, *Slavery to Freedom*, pp. 134-37.

A small number of Virginia Negroes, slaves as well as free-men, saw active military and naval service. In 1776, free mulattoes were permitted to serve as drummers, pipers, and pioneers, these being duties not normally requiring the bearing of arms.[28] A rumor that slaves could win freedom by fighting was also circulating, to such an extent that a 1777 law required recruiting officers to see that any Negro they enlisted could provide a certificate of freedom.[29] This law implies that free Negroes by then were being accepted for full military service.

A certain amount of illegal enlistment of slaves continued to go on throughout the war, in some cases because the rumor still persisted that freedom could be won and in others because slaveowners fraudulently represented them as freemen and then used them as substitutes for free white men.[30] Then, at the conclusion of the war, the owner expected to reclaim a Negro substitute as a slave.[31] The sordid character of this procedure influenced the legislature to vote in 1783 to free slaves who had been enlisted in this way.[32] A few special acts conferring freedom on slaves for meritorious service during the war were also passed in the 1780s. One of the more notable examples was James Armistead, who had been of conspicuous assistance to Lafayette.[33]

Many slaves in Virginia were already experienced boatmen and pilots long before the war with Great Britain had begun. A number of them were used to fill out the crews of Virginia naval vessels and in one case to command a vessel.[34]

The real importance of the American Revolution to the Negro was not, however, the limited opportunity it gave him to participate as a soldier. Rather it was the fact that large numbers of Americans for the first time began to grasp the inconsistency of slavery and the doctrines of natural rights on

---

28. Ibid., p. 134.

29. Hening, *Statutes*, 9: 280.

30. *Virginia Gazette* (Purdie), April 11, 1777.

31. *The Negro in Virginia*. Compiled by the Writers' Program of the Work Projects Administration (New York, 1940), pp. 23-24.

32. Hening, *Statutes*, 11: 308-9.

33. Ibid., 10: 115, 211, 372; 12: 380-81; 13: 102, 103, 618-20.

34. *Negro in Virginia*, p. 21; *Virginia Historical Register*, 1: 80, 129, 131.

which they had based their own struggle for political independence. How far the correction of this inconsistency progressed depended very closely upon geography. In the northern colonies the tide of revolutionary spirit swept away the very institution of slavery, and as far south as Virginia and North Carolina serious inroads were made before a reaction set in.[35]

Some of the individual leaders of the revolutionary movement in the colony, being more at home with theories of liberty and more aware of the demands of logic, began to nibble at the edges of the problem before 1776. In his celebrated defense of a mulatto indentured servant before the General Court in 1770, Jefferson had pleaded the universality of human freedom without qualification in an effort to end the man's obligated service.[36] Jefferson also recalled joining Richard Bland about this time in trying to win a moderate extension of legal protection to slaves.[37] Both these efforts came to nothing. Patrick Henry was on record in 1773 that slavery was "repugnant to humanity," though he admitted that he was a slaveholder himself, "drawn along by the general inconvenience of living without them."[38]

The work of the Virginia Convention of 1776 served to draw the lines between those who believed the implications of the American struggle for independence had to be carried out to the extent of abolishing slavery and those more cautious men who were troubled on this score neither by logic nor liberality. In the first article of the Declaration of Rights, with its unqualified assertion that "all men are by nature equally free," the issue was joined most clearly; so it is not surprising that there was debate on the relevance of this very point to slavery. Robert Carter Nicholas, and perhaps others, attacked the first article as

35. Ulrich B. Phillips, *American Negro Slavery* (New York, 1918), pp. 115-21; J. R. Brackett, "Status of Slave, 1775-1789," *Essays in Constitutional History*, edited by J. Franklin Jameson. (Boston and New York, 1889).

36. Dumas Malone, *Jefferson the Virginian* (Boston, 1948), pp. 121-22.

37. James E. Pate, "Richard Bland's Inquiry Into the Rights of the British Colonies," *William and Mary Quarterly*, 2nd ser., 11 (January, 1931): 20.

38. James Curtis Ballagh, *A History of Slavery in Virginia* (Baltimore, 1902), p. 130.

an invitation to "civil convulsion." The antislavery men certainly did not reveal their hands at this time, however, for they answered, "not without inconsistency" as Edmund Randolph observed, that slaves were not "constituent members" of society and could derive no benefit from the Virginia Declaration of Rights.[39]

There is no avoiding the fact that this refusal to admit the Negro might benefit from the Virginia Declaration of Rights was the majority view. It was not, however, the view of Mason, the author of that first article, or of Jefferson or George Wythe and of others who had kept silent during the debate. Nor was discussion of the relevance of slavery to the Revolution yet over. Jefferson and Wythe were named to the committee created that same summer to make a systematic revision of the laws of the commonwealth, and one of the tasks the two men set for themselves was to write a plan of emancipation into law.[40] And the issue continued to be debated elsewhere—in the meetings of Phi Beta Kappa and in the columns of the *Gazette*, where an opponent of slavery reminded an adversary ". . . to read with attention the first section of the declaration of rights, and to place his slaves in the situation so justly declared to be the natural right of all mankind, for 'till that be done the talk of justice is far from being completed. . . ."[41]

The impact of the American Revolution on the institution of slavery in Virginia by no means expended itself in the years between 1776 and 1783. It was a continuing movement which had some degree of vitality over the last two decades of the eighteenth century. Among those who sought to alleviate the position of Negroes within the new state three separate objectives became apparent: the prohibition of the overseas slave trade, the legalizing of private manumission, and the emancipation of slaves by public law. One of these was a complete success, one achieved momentary fulfillment, and the third ended in absolute failure.

39. Edmund Randolph, *History of Virginia,* edited by Arthur H. Shaffer (Charlottesville, Va., 1970), p. 253.
40. Phillips, *American Negro Slavery,* p. 122; Thomas Jefferson, *Notes on Virginia,* edited by William Peden (Chapel Hill, N.C., 1955), p. 137.
41. *William and Mary Quarterly,* 1st ser., 4: 225; *Virginia Gazette* (Dixon and Nicolson), April 1, 1780.

The importation of slaves from Africa had been in abeyance for two years before independence and under attack for much longer. Consequently, its permanent repeal by the legislature in 1778 caused no difficulty.[42] The new statute, in fact, applied not only to the overseas trade but to Negroes brought into Virginia by land as well, although there was a loophole to protect *bona fide* masters moving into the state with their Negroes. Slaves introduced into the state in violation of this law were entitled to freedom, and eventually, in 1795, the procedure by which a slave might bring suit for freedom under this law became relatively simple.[43]

Initially, sentiment was running fairly strongly in favor of permitting any master who cared to do so to free his slaves, even though this had been contrary to colonial practice. In a number of cases owners began to leave wills instructing that certain slaves be freed, though the law had not been altered to allow this.[44] But in the case of John Barr of Northumberland County the assembly proceeded to recognize such an act of manumission in 1777.[45] In other instances the assembly voted a number of years later to legalize such wills.[46]

The rewriting of the law to permit voluntary manumission without the danger of complications like these occurred in 1782.[47] Slaves so liberated were free to continue to reside within the state, the only real restriction being one which was placed on the former master, namely, to be financially responsible for freed Negroes who were too old or too young to support themselves. County records of the 1780s and 1790s contain numerous examples of wills in which masters took advantage of the new law.[48] Some obviously rewarded only a particularly

42. Hening, *Statutes*, 9: 471-72.
43. Ibid., 10: 307-8; 12: 182-83; Ballagh, *Slavery in Virginia*, pp. 123-24.
44. Ibid., p. 120.
45. Hening, *Statutes*, 9: 320-21.
46. Ibid., 12: 611-16.
47. Ibid., 11: 39-40.
48. For example, see York County Records, Wills and Inventories, Book 23, p. 685; Hening, *Statutes*, 11:362-63; *Virginia Magazine*, 2 (Oct., 1894): 210; 20 (Jan., 1912): 110; 24 (Jan., 1916): 73-74; 56 (July, 1948): 348-49; *William and Mary Quarterly*, 1st ser., 9 (July, 1900): 27n; 11 (Oct., 1902): 139.

faithful servant or two, others outlined comprehensive schemes which were designed to free all of their Negroes in stages over a period of years. Many heaped recriminations upon themselves and their fellows for having acted "in contradiction of their own declaration of Rights, and in violation of every sacred law of Nature." There are estimates which place the average number of manumissions at a thousand per year during the first decade in which the law was in force.[49]

The idealism and moral fervor which had produced this wave of voluntary manumissions was doomed to be short-lived; for there soon began to be a sharp reaction from owners who declined to free their own slaves and who found the new freemen a disruptive element in their localities. The experience of Robert Carter of Nomini Hall is a good example of what happened. Carter, whose motivation in so doing was primarily religious, but also partly economic, worked out in 1791 a scheme for gradually freeing his slaves, an undertaking rendered the more spectacular by the fact that he was one of the largest slaveholders in the colony with Negroes scattered out over many different landholdings. He proposed to begin by setting free thirty older slaves in 1791 with an additional number gaining their freedom every January 2 through the year 1812.[50] The flood of protests mounted steadily from planters living near lands on which some of the Negroes had been manumitted. One letter which came in anonymously from Frederick County complained that ". . . a man has almost as good a right to set fire to his own building though his neighbors is to be destroyed by it, as to free his slaves. . . ."[51]

Eventually the whole scheme broke down with Carter's death. His sons were not anxious to see it completed and probably only a small number of the Negroes ever really benefited.[52] Finally, protests similar to those which had poured in upon Robert Carter caused a revision of the 1782 law in 1805 that went back to colonial precedents and allowed owners to free

49. Ballagh, *Slavery in Virginia*, p. 121.

50. Louis Morton, *Robert Carter of Nomini Hall* (Williamsburg, Va., 1941), pp. 251-65.

51. Ibid., p. 266.

52. Ibid., pp. 268-69.

slaves only if the Negroes then left the state.[53] With this action the Revolution became a dead letter, so far as slavery in Virginia was concerned.

The third and most sweeping objective, the emancipation of Virginia's slaves, was never more than a straw in the wind. The motivation for seeking this arose not from the political principles of the Revolution alone but also from religious conviction, notably among the Quakers and some Baptists, and from more hard-headed economic reasoning that tobacco was bound to decline and render slave labor unprofitable. Singly or collectively, these remained, however, distinctly minority views.

In their work on the committee to revise the laws of the state Wythe and Jefferson evolved a plan for emancipation which they planned to introduce in the legislature of 1779. Briefly, they would have freed slaves born after the passage of the act, provided for their education in "tillage, arts or sciences," and then have arranged for their settlement outside the state. As it turned out, the two men did not even attempt to get consideration of their proposal.[54]

There were also some organized efforts from the Quakers, primarily petitions to the legislature. Before the voluntary manumission law of 1782, these had been appeals for recognition of the right of the Quakers to free their own Negroes. Subsequently there was at least one petition for general emancipation, during the session of 1785, but it was rejected by unanimous vote.[55]

Although a few men continued to hope, as Washington did, that slavery might "be abolished by slow, sure and imperceptible degrees," there was in reality only one other noteworthy effort to revive emancipation.[56] This was the appearance of St. George Tucker's *Dissertation on Slavery with a Proposal for the Gradual Abolition of It in the State of Virginia*, published and presented to the legislature in 1796, where it was promptly dismissed from consideration. Tucker reprinted it as an appendix to his edition of Blackstone in 1803, but emancipation as a

53. Helen T. Catterall, ed., *Judicial Cases Concerning American Slavery and the Negro* (Washington, 1924-1926), 1: 73-74.

54. Jefferson, *Notes on Virginia*, p. 137.

55. Brackett, "Status of Slave," pp. 303-7.

56. Phillips, *American Negro Slavery*, p. 123.

political issue did not really come alive again until the great debates of 1831-1832.[57]

Both the writings of Jefferson and Tucker, who had more to say about ending slavery than any other Virginians of this era, make it clear that even the minority who would have freed the slaves based their proposals on the assumption that emancipation had to be carried out gradually and that it had to include colonization. It was also obvious that they, no less than the defenders of slavery, regarded the Negro as an inferior being, incapable of assimilation into free society in Virginia.[58]

So far then as slavery and the Negro were concerned, the American Revolution offered in Virginia a few years of hope and little more.[59] The end of the overseas trade in 1778 and the recognition of voluntary manumission in 1782 marked a considerable beginning, but slavery proved to be a problem of such deep social and economic consequences as not to be susceptible to gradual solutions. In a few years Virginia's profitable export of Negroes in the domestic trade would replace the overseas commerce in human flesh. The right of an individual to free his own slaves was once again sharply restricted. And the emancipation movement, weak enough in any event, would be displaced by a colonization movement, doomed by its spirit of condescension and its impracticality.

57. Tucker's pamphlet is most readily available in Mrs. George P. Coleman, ed., *Virginia Silhouettes: Contemporary Letters Concerning Negro Slavery in the State of Virginia* (Richmond, Va., 1934), Appendix.

58. Tucker, *Dissertation on Slavery*, p. 51ff; Jefferson, *Notes on Virginia*, p. 138ff. Tucker simply quotes at length from Jefferson on this point, but this certainly indicates that both men agreed on the Negro's inferiority.

59. By looking at incidental changes prompted by the Revolution rather than focusing, as I have tended to do, on conscious political actions of the revolutionary leadership, Gerald W. Mullin, *Flight and Rebellion: Slave Resistance in Eighteenth-Century Virginia* (New York, 1972), Chs. 4, 5, is able to put the effect of the American Revolution on slavery in a somewhat different light, one that suggests its impact on the black population was very great, even though slavery itself did not cease. For slavery in the revolutionary and post-revolutionary period, see also Robert McColley, *Slavery and Jeffersonian Virginia* (Urbana, Ill., 1964); James Hugo Johnston, *Race Relations in Virginia & Miscegenation in the South, 1776-1860* (Amherst, Mass., 1970); and Winthrop D. Jordan, *White Over Black: American Attitudes Toward the Negro, 1550-1812* (Chapel Hill, N.C., 1968), parts 3-5.

CHAPTER XII

The Negro's Role in
Colonial Williamsburg: A Summary

W HEN ALL the evidence is in concerning the Negro population of eighteenth-century Williamsburg—and it is unfortunately
little enough information—perhaps what remains as the most
important single feature of the Negro's life here is the simple
fact that slaves were about half the resident population of the
capital. Because they were a subjugated, inarticulate, leaderless
half it becomes simple enough to forget how much they must
have influenced life in Williamsburg and all but impossible to
arrive at an adequate estimate of that influence.

Sooner or later every part of the civilization of colonial
Virginia bore the impress of slavery. It helped, for instance, to
build up the stratified society characteristic of Virginia; and at
the same time it partially destroyed the mobility that was also a
feature of this society. Some aspects of the life of the colony,
such as the organization of society, law, custom, or the place of
religion, are areas in which Williamsburg serves conveniently as
a specific example of what was largely true in the whole of the
Tidewater and Piedmont.

Economically, Williamsburg was neither so important nor so
typical. Lacking a share in the slave trade, not inhabited by
large numbers of field slaves, and possibly not even well
populated with Negro craftsmen, the town utilized its slaves
largely as domestics. This was a society, however, in which
household labor was important. Furthermore, slave property
undoubtedly comprised a significant proportion of Williamsburg's wealth.

It was in the life of the Negro himself that Williamsburg may
have been more distinctive. Here the slave seemed to be more
fully adjusted to white society, more skilled at domestic tasks,
to a degree better educated, and perhaps more restive under
the yoke of slavery than on the plantation. There should be
sober realism, however, about the hardship of the average

slave's life. Even in town, living conditions were almost certainly primitive and regimentation as strict as it could be made.

With consideration of the impact of the American Revolution on slavery, Williamsburg comes back into the mainstream of the development of Virginia, for the political battles fought and the political principles established here belong to the history of the whole colony and state, and indeed to the whole nation. In the matter of slavery, however, it must be admitted that, so far as the southern colonies were concerned, the spirit of the Revolution was at its least triumphant.

As a last word, we ought perhaps to come back to an extremely simple, unpretentious point, that is, how much the slaves were a part of the ordinary daily life of Williamsburg and how frequently they would have been seen at work, along the street, or perhaps on the fringes of some large public gathering.[1]

1. Again, the reader should see Gerald W. Mullin, *Flight and Rebellion: Slave Resistance in Eighteenth-Century Virginia* (New York, 1972), *passim*, for an account that casts the Negro in a somewhat less passive role than I may have implied.

A BIBLIOGRAPHY OF BLACKS IN COLONIAL VIRGINIA

The purpose of this bibliography is to provide a somewhat more extensive and up-to-date listing of works on the black history of early Virginia than those cited in the footnotes of this volume alone, but it is by no means intended to be comprehensive. It does include a reasonably complete listing of printed sources, bibliographical aids, books, and articles that relate specifically to blacks in Virginia before 1800, and a much more selective listing of similar printed materials that pertain more broadly to American black history in the eighteenth and nineteenth centuries and yet provide an important context in which to understand the specific example of Virginia. Studies of blacks in other British colonies are not, however, listed. For the seventh printing, the bibliography has been expanded to include work published through the spring of 1994.

Bibliographical Aids

Cappon, Lester J., and Stella F. Duff, comps. *Virginia Gazette Index, 1736–1780.* 2 vols. Williamsburg, Va.: Institute of Early American History and Culture, 1950.

Swem, E. G., comp. *Virginia Historical Index.* 2 vols. Roanoke, Va.: Stone Printing and Manufacturing Co., 1934.

Printed Sources

Billings, Warren M. "The Cases of Fernando and Elizabeth Key: A Note on the Status of Blacks in Seventeenth-Century Virginia." *William and Mary Quarterly,* 3rd Ser., XXX (1973), pp. 467–474.

Coleman, Mrs. George P., ed. *Virginia Silhouettes: Contemporary Letters Concerning Negro Slavery in the State of Virginia.* Richmond, Va.: Dietz Press, 1934.

Evans, Emory G., ed. "A Question of Complexion: Documents Concerning the Negro and the Franchise in Eighteenth-Century Virginia." *Virginia Magazine of History and Biography,* LXXI (1963), pp. 411–415.

Jefferson, Thomas. *Notes on the State of Virginia.* Edited by William Peden. Chapel Hill, N. C.: University of North Carolina Press, 1955.

Maxwell, William. "Smyth's Travels in Virginia, in 1773." *Virginia Historical Register,* VI (1853), pp. 11–20, 77–90, 131–148.

Minchinton, Walter, Celia King, and Peter Waite, eds. *Virginia Slave-*

Trade Statistics, 1698–1775. Richmond, Va.: Virginia State Library, 1984.

Perry, William Stevens, ed. *Historical Collections Relating to the American Colonial Church,* Vol. 1. Hartford, Conn.: Printed for the Subscribers, 1870.

Schmidt, Fredrika Teute, and Barbara Ripel Wilhelm. "Early Pro-slavery Petitions in Virginia." *William and Mary Quarterly,* 3rd Ser., XXX (1973), pp. 133–146.

United States Bureau of the Census. *Heads Of Families At The First Census Of The United States Taken In The Year 1790: Records Of The State Enumerations: 1781–1785: Virginia.* Washington, D. C.: U. S. Government Printing Office, 1908.

Van Horne, John C., ed. *Religious Philanthropy and Colonial Slavery: The American Correspondence of the Associates of Dr. Bray, 1717–1777.* Urbana, Ill.: University of Illinois Press, 1985.

Windley, Lathan A., comp. *Runaway Slave Advertisements: A Documentary History from the 1730's to 1790.* Volume 1: *Virginia and North Carolina.* Westport, Conn.: Greenwood Press, 1983.

Virginia Gazette. [Williamsburg], 1736–1780.

Books

Ames, Susie M. *Studies of the Virginia Eastern Shore in the Seventeenth Century.* Richmond, Va.: Dietz Press, 1940.

Ballagh, James Curtis. *A History of Slavery in Virginia.* Baltimore: Johns Hopkins University Press, 1902.

Berkeley, Francis L., Jr. *Dunmore's Proclamation of Emancipation.* Charlottesville, Va.: University Press of Virginia, 1941.

Boskin, Joseph. *Into Slavery: Racial Decisions in the Virginia Colony.* Philadelphia: J. B. Lippincott, 1976.

Breen, T. H., and Stephen Innes. *"Myne Owne Ground": Race and Freedom on Virginia's Eastern Shore, 1640–1676.* New York: Oxford University Press, 1980.

Cope, Robert S. *Carry Me Back: Slavery and Servitude in Seventeenth-Century Virginia.* Pikesville, Ky.: Pikesville College Press of the Appalachian Studies Center, 1973.

Craven, Wesley Frank. *The Southern Colonies in the Seventeenth Century, 1607–1689.* Baton Rouge, La.: Louisiana State University Press, 1949.

——. *White, Red, and Black: The Seventeenth-Century Virginian.* Charlottesville, Va.: University Press of Virginia, 1971.

Deal, Joseph Douglass. *Race and Class in Colonial Virginia: Indians, Englishmen, and Africans on the Eastern Shore during the Seventeenth Century.* New York: Garland Publishing, 1993.

Earnest, Joseph B., Jr. *The Religious Development of the Negro in Virginia*. Charlottesville, Va.: Michie Co., 1914.

Egerton, Douglas R. *Gabriel's Rebellion: The Virginia Slave Conspiracies of 1800 and 1802*. Chapel Hill, N. C.: University of North Carolina Press, 1993.

Isaac, Rhys. *The Transformation of Virginia, 1740–1790*. Chapel Hill, N. C.: University of North Carolina Press, 1982.

Johnston, James Hugo. *Race Relations in Virginia & Miscegenation in the South, 1776–1860*. Amherst, Mass.: University of Massachusetts Press, 1970.

Klein, Herbert S. *Slavery in the Americas: A Comparative Study of Virginia and Cuba*. Chicago: University of Chicago Press, 1967.

Kulikoff, Allan. *Tobacco and Slaves: The Development of Southern Culture in the Chesapeake, 1680–1800*. Chapel Hill, N. C.: University of North Carolina Press, 1986.

Lewis, Ronald L. *Coal, Iron, and Slaves: Industrial Slavery in Maryland and Virginia, 1715–1865*. Westport, Conn.: Greenwood Press, 1979.

McColley, Robert. *Slavery and Jeffersonian Virginia*. Urbana, Ill.: University of Illinois Press, 1964.

Morgan, Edmund S. *American Slavery, American Freedom: The Ordeal of Colonial Virginia*. New York: W. W. Norton & Co., 1975.

Morgan, Philip D., ed. *"Don't Grieve After Me": The Black Experience in Virginia, 1619–1986*. Hampton, Va.: Hampton University, 1986.

Mullin, Gerald W. *Flight and Rebellion: Slave Resistance in Eighteenth-Century Virginia*. New York: Oxford University Press, 1972.

Perry, James R. *The Formation of a Society on Virginia's Eastern Shore, 1615–1655*. Chapel Hill, N. C.: University of North Carolina Press, 1990.

Pinchbeck, Raymond B. "The Virginia Negro Artisan and Tradesman." *Publications of the University of Virginia Phelps-Stokes Fellowship Papers*, No. 7. Richmond, Va.: William Byrd Press, 1926.

Russell, John H. *The Free Negro in Virginia, 1619–1865*. Baltimore: Johns Hopkins University Press, 1913.

Rutman, Darrett B., and Anita H. Rutman. *A Place in Time: Middlesex County, Virginia, 1650–1750*. New York: W. W. Norton & Co., 1984.

Schwarz, Philip J. *Twice Condemned: Slaves and the Criminal Laws of Virginia, 1705–1865*. Baton Rouge, La.: Louisiana State University Press, 1988.

Sobel, Mechal. *The World They Made Together: Black and White*

Values in Eighteenth-Century Virginia. Princeton, N. J.: Princeton University Press, 1987.

Writers' Program of the Works Progress Administration in the State of Virginia. *The Negro in Virginia.* New York: Hastings House, 1940.

Articles

Allen, Theodore. " '. . . They Would Have Destroyed Me': Slavery and the Origins of Racism." *Radical America,* IX (1975), pp. 41–63.

Bailor, Keith M. "John Taylor of Caroline: Continuity, Change, and Discontinuity in Virginia's Sentiments toward Slavery, 1790–1820." *Virginia Magazine of History and Biography,* LXXV (1967), pp. 290–304.

Beeman, Richard R. "Labor Forces and Race Relations: A Comparative View of the Colonization of Brazil and Virginia." *Political Science Quarterly,* LXXXVI (1971), pp. 609–636.

Bernhard, Virginia. "Beyond the Chesapeake: The Contrasting Status of Blacks in Bermuda, 1616–1663." *Journal of Southern History,* LIV (1988), pp. 545–564.

Billings, Warren M. "The Law of Servants and Slaves in Seventeenth-Century Virginia." *Virginia Magazine of History and Biography,* XCIX (1991), pp. 45–62.

Bowman, Larry G. "Virginia's Use of Blacks in the French and Indian War." *Western Pennsylvania Historical Magazine,* LIII (1970), pp. 57–63.

Breen, T. H. "A Changing Labor Force and Race Relations in Virginia, 1660–1710." *Journal of Social History,* VII (1973), pp. 3–25.

Brewer, James H. "Negro Property Owners in Seventeenth-Century Virginia." *William and Mary Quarterly,* 3rd Ser., XII (1955), pp. 575–580.

Craven, Wesley Frank. "Twenty Negroes to Jamestown in 1619?" *Virginia Quarterly Review,* XLVII (1971), pp. 416–420.

Degler, Carl N. "Slavery and the Genesis of American Race Prejudice." *Comparative Studies in Society and History,* II (1959), pp. 49–66.

Dunn, Richard S. "Black Society in the Chesapeake, 1776–1810." In Ira Berlin and Ronald Hoffman, eds., *Slavery and Freedom in the Age of the American Revolution,* pp. 49–82. Charlottesville, Va.: University Press of Virginia, 1983.

———. "Masters, Servants, and Slaves in the Colonial Chesapeake and the Caribbean." In David B. Quinn, ed., *Early Maryland in a Wider World,* pp. 242–266. Detroit, Mich.: Wayne State University Press, 1982.

Frey, Sylvia R. "Between Slavery and Freedom: Virginia Blacks in the American Revolution." *Journal of Southern History*, XLIX (1983), pp. 375–398.

Goodwin, Mary S. "Christianizing and Educating the Negro in Colonial Virginia." *Historical Magazine of the Protestant Episcopal Church*, I (1932), pp. 143–152.

Greenberg, Michael. "William Byrd II and the World of the Market." *Southern Studies*, XVI (1977), pp. 429–456.

Gundersen, Joan Rezner. "The Double Bonds of Race and Sex: Black and White Women in a Colonial Virginia Parish." *Journal of Southern History*, LII (1986), pp. 351–372.

Handlin, Oscar, and Mary F. Handlin. "Origins of the Southern Labor System." *William and Mary Quarterly*, 3rd Ser., VII (1950), pp. 199–222.

Hast, Adele. "The Legal Status of the Negro in Virginia, 1705–1765." *Journal of Negro History*, LIV (1969), pp. 217–239.

Hughes, Sarah S. "Slaves for Hire: The Allocation of Black Labor in Elizabeth City County, Virginia, 1782–1810." *William and Mary Quarterly*, 3rd Ser., XXXV (1978), pp. 260–286.

Isaac, Rhys. "Communication and Control: Authority Metaphors and Power Contests on Colonel Landon Carter's Virginia Plantation, 1752–1778." In Sean Wilentz, ed., *Rites of Power: Symbolism, Ritual, and Politics since the Middle Ages*, pp. 275–302. Philadelphia: University of Pennsylvania Press, 1985.

Jackson, Luther P. "Religious Development of the Negro in Virginia from 1760 to 1860." *Journal of Negro History*, XVI (1931), pp. 168–239.

———. "Virginia Negro Soldiers and Seamen in the American Revolution." *Journal of Negro History*, XXVII (1942), pp. 247–287.

Jones, Jerome W. "The Established Virginia Church and the Conversion of Negroes and Indians, 1620–1760." *Journal of Negro History*, XLVI (1961), pp. 12–23.

Klein, Herbert S. "Slaves and Shipping in Eighteenth-Century Virginia." *Journal of Interdisciplinary History*, V (1975), pp. 383–412.

Kulikoff, Allan. "The Origins of Afro-American Society in Tidewater Maryland and Virginia, 1700 to 1790." *William and Mary Quarterly*, 3rd Ser., XXXV (1978), pp. 226–259.

———. "A 'Prolifick' People: Black Population Growth in the Chesapeake Colonies, 1700–1790." *Southern Studies*, XVI (1977), pp. 391–428.

Lee, Jean Butenhoff. "The Problem of Slave Community in the Eighteenth-Century Chesapeake." *William and Mary Quarterly*, 3rd Ser., XLIII (1986), pp. 333–361.

Lewis, Ronald L. "Slavery on Chesapeake Iron Plantations before the American Revolution." *Journal of Negro History*, LIX (1984), pp. 242–254.

———. "The Use and Extent of Slave Labor in the Chesapeake Iron Industry: The Colonial Era." *Labor History*, XVII (1976), pp. 388–405.

MacMaster, Richard K. "Arthur Lee's 'Address on Slavery': An Aspect of Virginia's Struggle to End the Slave Trade, 1765–1774." *Virginia Magazine of History and Biography*, LXXX (1971), pp. 141–157.

Menard, Russell. "From Servants to Slaves: The Transformation of the Chesapeake Labor System." *Southern Studies*, XVI (1977), pp. 355–390.

Morgan, Philip D. "Slave Life in Piedmont Virginia, 1720–1780." In Lois Green Carr, Philip D. Morgan, and Jean B. Russo, eds., *Colonial Chesapeake Society*, pp. 433–484. Chapel Hill, N. C.: University of North Carolina Press, 1988.

———. "Three Planters and Their Slaves: Perspectives on Slavery in Virginia, South Carolina, and Jamaica, 1750–1790." In Winthrop D. Jordan and Sheila L. Skemp, eds., *Race and Family in the Colonial South*, pp. 37–79. Jackson, Miss.: University Press of Mississippi, 1987.

Morgan, Philip D., and Michael L. Nicholls. "Slaves in Piedmont Virginia, 1720–1790." *William and Mary Quarterly*, 3rd Ser., XLVI (1989), pp. 211–251.

Nicholls, Michael L. "Passing Through This Troublesome World: Free Blacks in the Early Southside." *Virginia Magazine of History and Biography*, XCII (1984), pp. 50–70.

Palmer, Paul D. "Servant into Slave: The Evolution of the Legal Status of the Negro Laborer in Colonial Virginia." *South Atlantic Quarterly*, LXV (1966), pp. 355–370.

Pennington, Edgar Legare. "Thomas Bray's Associates and their Work among Negroes." *American Antiquarian Society Proceedings*, New Ser., XLVIII (1938), pp. 311–403.

Pilcher, George William. "Samuel Davies and the Instruction of Negroes in Virginia." *Virginia Magazine of History and Biography*, LXXIV (1966), pp. 293–300.

Quarles, Benjamin. "Lord Dunmore as Liberator." *William and Mary Quarterly*, 3rd Ser., XV (1958), pp. 494–507.

Russell, John H. "Colored Freemen as Slave Owners in Virginia." *Journal of Negro History*, I (1916), pp. 233–242.

Schwarz, Philip J. " 'A Sense of Their Own Power': Self-Determination in Recent Writing on Black Virginians." *Virginia Magazine of History and Biography*, XCVII (1989), pp. 279–310.

————. "Slaves and Crime in Late Eighteenth-Century Virginia." *Virginia Magazine of History and Biography*, XC (1982), pp. 283–309.

Shammas, Carol. "Black Women's Work and the Evolution of Plantation Society in Virginia." *Labor History*, XXVI (1985), pp. 5–28.

Stealey, John Edward, III. "The Responsibilities and Liabilities of the Bailee of Slave Labor in Virginia." *American Journal of Legal History*, XII (1968), pp. 336–353.

Sweig, Donald M. "The Importation of African Slaves to the Potomac River, 1732–1772." *William and Mary Quarterly*, 3rd Ser., XLII (1985), pp. 507–524.

Vaughan, Alden T. "Blacks in Virginia: A Note on the First Decade." *William and Mary Quarterly*, 3rd Ser., XXIX (1972), pp. 469–478.

————. "The Origins Debate: Slavery and Racism in Seventeenth-Century Virginia." *Virginia Magazine of History and Biography*, XCVII (1989), pp. 311–354.

Vlach, John Michael. "Afro-American Domestic Artifacts in Eighteenth-Century Virginia." *Material Culture*, XIX (1987), pp. 3–23.

Wax, Darold D. "Negro Import Duties in Colonial Virginia: A Story of British Commercial Policy and Local Public Policy." *Virginia Magazine of History and Biography*, LXXIX (1971), pp. 29–45.

Westbury, Susan. "Slaves of Colonial Virginia: Where They Came From." *William and Mary Quarterly*, 3rd Ser., XLII (1985), pp. 228–237.

RELATED WORK IN BLACK HISTORY

Biographical Aids

Berlin, Ira. "Time, Space, and the Evolution of Afro-American Society in British Mainland North America." *American Historical Review*, LXXXV (1980), pp. 44–78.

Catterall, Helen T., ed. *Judicial Cases concerning American Slavery and the Negro*. 5 vols. Washington, D. C.: Carnegie Institution, 1924–1926.

Donnan, Elizabeth, ed. *Documents Illustrative of the History of the Slave Trade to America*. Vol. 4: *The Border Colonies and the*

Southern Colonies. Washington, D. C.: Carnegie Institution, 1935.

Howe, Mentor A., and Roscoe E. Lewis, comps. *A Classified Catalog of the Negro Collection in the Collis P. Huntington Library, Hampton Institute.* Hampton, Va.: Hampton Institute, 1940.

Miller, Elizabeth W., comp. *The Negro in America: A Bibliography.* Cambridge, Mass.: Harvard University Press, 1966.

Sensbach, Jon F. "Charting a Course in Early African-American History." *William and Mary Quarterly*, 3rd Ser., L (1993), pp. 394–405.

United States Bureau of the Census. *Historical Statistics of the United States: Colonial Times to 1957.* Washington, D. C.: U. S. Government Printing Office, 1960.

Wood, Peter H. " 'I Did the Best I Could for My Day': The Study of Early Black History during the Second Reconstruction, 1960 to 1976." *William and Mary Quarterly*, 3rd Ser., XXXV (1978), pp. 185–225.

Work, Monroe N., comp. *Bibliography of the Negro in Africa and America.* New York: H. W. Wilson Company, 1928.

Books

Berlin, Ira. *Slaves Without Masters: The Free Negro in the Antebellum South.* New York: Random House, 1974.

Berlin, Ira, and Ronald Hoffman, eds. *Slavery and Freedom in the Age of the American Revolution.* Charlottesville, Va.: University Press of Virginia, 1983.

Berlin, Ira, and Philip D. Morgan, eds. *The Slaves' Economy: Independent Production by Slaves in the Americas.* London: Frank Cass & Co., 1991.

Blassingame, John W. *The Slave Community: Plantation Life in the Antebellum South.* New York: Oxford University Press, 1972.

Curtin, Philip D. *The Atlantic Slave Trade: A Census.* Madison, Wis.: University of Wisconsin Press, 1969.

Dalzell, George W. *Benefit of Clergy in America & Related Matters.* Winston-Salem, N. C.: John F. Blair, 1955.

Davies, Kenneth G. *The Royal African Company.* New York: Longmans, Green and Co., 1957.

Davis, David Brion. *The Problem of Slavery in the Age of Revolution, 1770–1823.* Ithaca, N. Y.: Cornell University Press, 1975.

———. *The Problem of Slavery in Western Culture.* Ithaca, N. Y.: Cornell University Press, 1966.

———. *Slavery and Human Progress.* New York: Oxford University Press, 1984.

Dillon, Merton L. *Slavery Attacked: Southern Slaves and Their Allies, 1619–1865.* Baton Rouge, La.: Louisiana State University Press, 1990.

Ferguson, Leland. *Uncommon Ground: Archaeology and Early African America, 1650–1800.* Washington, D. C.: Smithsonian Institution Press, 1992.

Fogel, Robert William, and Stanley L. Engerman. *Time on the Cross: The Economics of American Negro Slavery.* Boston: Little, Brown, 1974.

Franklin, John Hope. *From Slavery to Freedom: A History of American Negroes.* New York: Alfred A. Knopf, 1948.

Frazier, E. Franklin. *The Negro in the United States.* New York: Macmillan, 1949.

Frey, Sylvia R. *Water from the Rock: Black Resistance in a Revolutionary Age.* Princeton, N. J.: Princeton University Press, 1991.

Genovese, Eugene D. *Roll, Jordan, Roll: The World The Slaves Made.* New York: Pantheon Books, 1974.

Gray, Lewis Cecil. *History of Agriculture in the Southern United States to 1860.* 2 vols. New York: Peter Smith, 1941.

Gutman, Herbert G. *The Black Family in Slavery and Freedom, 1750–1925.* New York: Pantheon Books, 1976.

Higginbotham, A. Leon, Jr. *In the Matter of Color: Race and the American Legal Process: The Colonial Period.* New York: Oxford University Press, 1978.

Huggins, Nathan Irvin. *Black Odyssey: The Afro-American Ordeal in Slavery.* New York: Pantheon Books, 1977.

Jordan, Winthrop D. *White Over Black: American Attitudes Toward the Negro, 1550–1812.* Chapel Hill, N. C.: University of North Carolina Press, 1968.

MacLeod, Duncan J. *Slavery, Race And The American Revolution.* New York: Cambridge University Press, 1974.

Phillips, Ulrich Bonnell. *American Negro Slavery, A Survey of the Supply, Employment and Control of Negro Labor as Determined by the Plantation Regime.* New York: D. Appleton & Co., 1918.

Quarles, Benjamin. *The Negro in the American Revolution.* Chapel Hill, N. C.: University of North Carolina Press, 1961.

Raboteau, Albert J. *Slave Rebellion: The "Invisible Institution" in the Antebellum South.* New York: Oxford University Press, 1978.

Tise, Larry E. *Proslavery: A History of the Defense of Slavery in America, 1701–1840.* Athens, Ga.: University of Georgia Press, 1987.

Toppin, Edgar A. *A Biographical History of Blacks in America Since 1528.* New York: David McKay, 1971.

Articles

Brackett, J. R. "Status of Slave, 1775–1789." In J. Franklin Jameson, ed., *Essays in Constitutional History of the United States in the Formative Period 1775–1789*. Boston: Houghton, Mifflin and Co., 1889.

Jernegan, Marcus W. "Slavery and Conversion in the American Colonies." *American Historical Review*, XXI (1916), pp. 504–527.

Jordan, Winthrop D. "Modern Tensions and the Origins of American Slavery." *Journal of Southern History*, XXVIII (1962), pp. 18–30.

Morgan, Edmund S. "Slavery and Freedom: The American Paradox." *Journal of American History*, LIX (1972), pp. 5–29.

Morgan, Philip D. "British Encounters with Africans and African-Americans, circa 1600–1780." In Bernard Bailyn and Philip D. Morgan, eds., *Strangers within the Realm: Cultural Margins of the First British Empire*, pp. 157–219. Chapel Hill, N. C.: University of North Carolina Press, 1991.

————. "Task and Gang Systems: The Organization of Labor on New World Plantations." In Stephen Innes, ed., *Work and Labor in Early America*, pp. 189–220. Chapel Hill, N. C.: University of North Carolina Press, 1988.

Mullin, Michael. "British Caribbean and North American Slaves in an Era of War and Revolution, 1775–1807." In Jeffrey J. Crow and Larry E. Tise, eds., *The Southern Experience in the American Revolution*, pp. 235–263. Chapel Hill, N. C.: University of North Carolina Press, 1978.

————. "Slave Obeahmen and Slaveowning Patriarchs in an Era of War and Revolution (1776–1807)." In Vera Rubin and Arthur Tuden, eds., *Comparative Perspectives on Slavery in New World Plantation Societies (Annals of the New York Academy of Sciences, Vol. 292)*, pp. 481–490. New York: New York Academy of Sciences, 1977.

Read, Allen W. "The Speech of Negroes in Colonial America." *Journal of Negro History*, XXIV (1939), pp. 247–258.

Wax, Darold D. "Preferences for Slaves in Colonial America." *Journal of Negro History*, LVIII (1973), pp. 371–401.

Wiecek, William W. "The Statutory Laws of Slavery and Race in the Thirteen Mainland Colonies of British America." *William and Mary Quarterly*, 3rd Ser., XXXIV (1977), pp. 258–280. [And Communication from Jeffrey J. Crow. *William and Mary Quarterly*, 3rd Ser., XXXIV (1977), pp. 695–697.]

Index